B-25 MITCHELL

A DETAIL & SCALE AVIATION PUBLICATION

in detail

Bert Kinzey

squadron/signal publications

COPYRIGHT © 1999 BY DETAIL & SCALE, INC.

This book is a product of Detail & Scale, Inc., which has sole responsibility for its content and layout, except that all contributors are responsible for the security clearance and copyright release of all materials submitted. Published by Squadron/Signal Publications, 1115 Crowley Drive, Carrollton, Texas 75011.

CONTRIBUTORS AND SOURCES:

Stan Piet	Stan Parker	U. S. Air Force Museum, Dayton, Ohio
Lloyd Jones	Bob Bartolacci	Museum of Aviation, Warner Robins, Georgia
Jim Roeder	Steve Benstead	U. S. Marine Corps Museum, Quantico, Virginia
Norman Avery	Carl Scholl	U. S. Navy
Bill Klaers	Tony Ritzman	U. S. Marine Corps
Bill Paul	Aero Trader	Rockwell International
Jim Galloway	National Archives	IPMS Spruce Goose Chapter

Detail & Scale, Inc. and the author express sincere appreciation to Mr. Robert Spaulding and his volunteers at the United States Air Force Museum at Dayton, Ohio, for their assistance in photographing the B-25D on display there. Mr. David Menard in the Research Division also provided valuable assistance, and without the use of the Research Division's excellent photographs and manuals, this publication would not have been possible.

A special word of thanks is also extended to Mr. Bill Klaers, pilot and owner of *In The Mood*, a beautifully rebuilt flying B-25J Mitchell. Mr. Klaers permitted several important photographs of his B-25J to be taken for use in this book

Mr. Carl Scholl of Aero Trader was also very helpful in providing technical information that we could not obtain from any other source. He pointed out small but important physical differences between Mitchell variants, and these were essential in the development of the most accurate scale drawings ever published of the B-25. This information also was used in the captions and text, and the author expresses special appreciation to Mr. Scholl for his valuable assistance.

Mr. Bill Paul of the Museum of Aviation at Warner Robins, Georgia, also deserves recognition for assisting the author with photography of the museum's B-25J and its Bendix A-9 gun turret.

Many photographs in this publication are credited to their contributors. Photographs with no credit indicated were taken by the author.

ISBN 1-888974-13-3

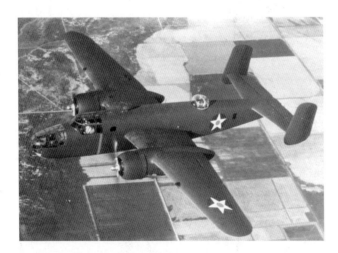

Above, front cover photo: Lacking any armament, the first B-25B flies over southern California during an early flight which was made so that North American could take publicity photographs of the new Mitchell variant.
(Rockwell)

Right, rear cover photo: Details inside the nose of a PBJ-1H are revealed as personnel perform maintenance on the armament and engines. (Varga via Piet)

INTRODUCTION

With its mid-mounted gull wings, oval fuselage cross section, under-wing engine nacelles, and twin vertical tails, North American's B-25 Mitchell medium bomber could not be mistaken for any other aircraft. This late production B-25J has the four external bomb racks under the outer wing panels. *(USAFM)*

On April 18, 1942, North American's B-25 Mitchell medium bomber flew into history as Lt. Col. James Doolittle led sixteen B-25Bs on one of the most famous raids in military history. Taking off from USS HORNET, CV-8, these aircraft struck the Japanese homeland for the first time in World War II, and although the raid did relatively little damage, its impact on the war cannot be overstated. It boosted the morale of American military personnel and civilians alike, and it made the Japanese realize that they were not invulnerable to attack, even in the city of Tokyo. It foreshadowed the massive raids by B-29s which would follow two and a half years later that would bring Japan to its knees and force a surrender.

Even if the Doolittle raid had never been flown, the B-25 would still have been the best known and most important medium bomber of the war. Although it was used extensively in the bombing role for which it was designed, it was even more effective as an attack aircraft in low level strafing attacks using large numbers of machine guns to obliterate targets on land and the surface of the sea. Two versions, the B-25G and B-25H, were also fitted with 75-mm cannon to make them even more formidable in this role.

Eight production versions rolled off the assembly lines, but the Mitchell was also one of the most modified aircraft of the war. Offensive and defensive armament was often enhanced at modification centers, field depots, and even by operational units. Because the number of post-production modifications made to the basic airframe ran into the hundreds, and because many of these were never even officially documented, it is impossible to discuss and illustrate each of them. However, the focus of this publication is to explain and depict all of the major changes made between one production variant and the next. The primary modifications made at depots and in the field are also discussed and are illustrated in photographs and drawings. Many of the differences between production variants and some of the important modifica-

tions have never been pointed out in any previous publication.

In reviewing reference material on the Mitchell, it was discovered that there were no accurate scale drawings available. Features from one variant to the next were sometimes mixed, and the shape of the airframe was often misrepresented. As a result, aviation researcher Lloyd Jones created an extensive set of new drawings specifically for this book. Technical drawings by North American, dimension data from manuals, and measurements on actual aircraft were all used to make these the most accurate scale drawings ever made available to the public. On them, we have indicated important changes that took place as the Mitchell variants were developed and produced during World War II. Because of the B-25's size, we were not able to reproduce those drawings at our usual 1/72nd scale, but we printed them as large as possible at 1/120th scale.

Because of its popularity and importance to the war effort, many references on the B-25 are presently available, but some of them rely heavily on rebuilt aircraft for both general and detailed photographs. Unfortunately, many features on these aircraft are not as they were when the Mitchell was in service. Some publications mistakenly illustrate and describe features that were quite different during World War II. This problem seems to be more significant and prevalent on the Mitchell than for any other aircraft Detail & Scale, Inc. has researched. Although it is necessary to use some detailed photographs of present-day B-25s, it is important to keep this to a minimum and use only details that are accurate and consistent with original production standards. In preparing for this publication, the author searched extensively for original photographs of cockpit interiors, gun positions, and other details that are usually no longer accurately represented on existing aircraft. Many such vintage photographs of the B-25's details have been included on the pages that follow. No general photographs of rebuilt B-25s are used in this book.

Research and preparation for this volume was more difficult than for most books in this series, and the extensive coverage would not have been possible without the assistance of many people and organizations that made significant contributions. Their names are listed on the previous page, and the author and Detail & Scale. Inc. express sincere appreciation for their help.

HISTORICAL SUMMARY

North American's model NA-40 was the sire of the B-25. The two shared common design features, including a tricycle landing gear, engine nacelles mounted under the wings, and twin vertical tails.   (Jones collection)

Early in 1936, the U. S. Army Air Corps issued a request for design proposals for a new twin-engine medium bomber. Among other things, the request for proposals specified that the aircraft had to be able to carry up to an 8,800 pound bomb load, have a top speed of 225 miles-per-hour, and a ceiling of 25,000 feet. With a 2,200-pound bomb load, combat range was to be 2,000 miles.

Although it had never produced a bomber design previously, North American Aviation developed its Model NA-21 in response to the request for proposals. Powered by two Pratt & Whitney R-1830 Twin Wasp powerplants, the NA-21 met or exceeded the specifications set forth in the request. Most notably, it could carry up to 10,000 pounds of bombs inside its bomb bay. On January 1, 1937, the NA-21 took off from the runway at North American's new plant at Inglewood, California. It was co-located with what was then called Mines Field, but today it is known as Los Angeles International Airport or LAX.

After subsequent testing of the NA-21 at Wright Army Air Field near Dayton, Ohio, the Army Air Corps concluded that the aircraft was underpowered, and the competing Douglas design was chosen. This design would enter production as the B-18 Bolo. However, this setback did not spell the end of the NA-21 nor North American's investment in a twin-engine medium bomber.

A revised design included a change in engines to the Pratt & Whitney R-2180 which significantly boosted the available horsepower. At North American, the aircraft was called Model NA-39, but the Army designated it the XB-21 Dragon. In spite of the new powerplants and other refinements in the design, the XB-21 still could not match the B-18 in performance or cost. As a result, it was finally eliminated from any further consideration. At this point, the only thing North American had to show for its efforts was the experience it had gained in designing a twin-engine medium bomber.

Even before the XB-21 was officially eliminated from consideration by the USAAC, North American was already working on a design for a twin-engine light attack bomber in response to another request for proposals issued on January 18, 1938. A single Model NA-40 was designed and built completely with company funds. When readied for its first flight in early 1939, it exhibited features quite different from the XB-21. These included a tricycle landing gear which could be fully retracted and covered by doors, mid-mounted wings with engine nacelles slung beneath them, and twin vertical tails. The pilot and co-pilot were seated in tandem under a long greenhouse style canopy, a design feature that North American's engineers believed would help streamline the airframe and reduce drag. As first flown, it was powered by two Pratt & Whitney R-1830 Twin Wasp engines which were uprated versions of the powerplants originally installed in the NA-21.

The performance of the NA-40 was less than satisfactory, so Wright R-2600-A71 Cyclone engines were installed in place of the Pratt & Whitney R-1830s. This new powerplant was a twin-row radial design with fourteen cylinders. With turbosupercharging, it could produce 1,350 horsepower at 15,000 feet, and 1,500 horsepower was provided for take off. As a result of this important improvement, the design number was changed to NA-40B. Flight testing immediately confirmed that performance had been increased considerably, and the NA-40B reached a top speed of 285 miles per hour. Just when everything was going well for the program, the aircraft crashed and was destroyed on April 11, 1939, just five weeks after its first flight. Unable to wait for another NA-40B to be built, the Army opted to purchase the competing Douglas model DB-7 instead. This design was produced as the A-20 Havoc light attack bomber.

On March 11, 1939, only eight days after the NA-40's first flight, the Army issued another request for proposals (Circular Proposal Number 39-640) calling for a five-place medium bombardment airplane. Using many features of the NA-40, North American quickly developed Model NA-62. On August 10, 1939, the Army announced a contract for 184 Model NA-62s which it designated the B-25.

By this time, the wars in Europe and Asia were esca-

The first production B-25 was not painted in the standard Olive Drab and Neutral Gray camouflage scheme like subsequent Mitchells, and it flew with several different designs for the vertical tails. It is most often associated with these tails which were smaller than that used on later B-25s. *(USAFM)*

lating, and it appeared to be only a matter of time before the United States would become involved. To expedite matters, the U. S. Army dispensed with the usual XB-25 and YB-25 experimental and prototype aircraft. The first production B-25-NAs would be used for testing as the subsequent aircraft were moving down the assembly line.

The fuselage of the aircraft was divided into four sections. In the nose was the bombardier's compartment which was reached through a crawlway running under the cockpit on the left side of the fueslage. Although an escape hatch for emergency egress was provided on the

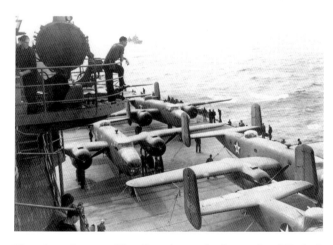

The American public first learned about the Mitchell when sixteen B-25Bs were flown from USS HORNET, CV-8, on a raid against Japan on April 18, 1942. The tail of the aircraft in the lower right corner of this photograph is that of the "RUPTURED DUCK," which was piloted by Lt. Ted W. Lawson. A color side profile of this aircraft appears on page 33. These B-25Bs did not have yellow tips on their propellers. *(National Archives)*

left side of the glass nose, it was practically useless in flight, because it was next to the propeller for the left engine. To safely get out of the aircraft during an in-flight emergency or in the event the aircraft was fatally hit by enemy fire, the bombardier had to crawl back through the passageway then exit through the lower hatch in the fuselage.

Behind the nose section was the cockpit which featured side by side seating for the pilot and co-pilot. Immediately aft of it was the navigator's compartment. The wing box and bomb bay formed the rear of the navigator's station, and above it was a crawlway leading back to the radio operator's compartment located immediately aft of the wing and bomb bay in the rear fuselage. The radio operator also had the responsibility of manning the waist guns and the cameras which were mounted in the aft fuselage.

At the rear of the B-25-NA was a rather large tail gun position which could be occupied by a gunner in the sitting, kneeling, or prone positions. This basic layout remained the same for all B-25 variants with only a few exceptions. The B-25G and B-25H had solid noses with no bombardier's compartment, and the same was true for some B-25Js which were fitted with the eight-gun solid nose. The B-25B, C, D, and G versions did not have tail gun positions as production standards, although some of these aircraft had them installed at modification centers and depots.

The first twenty-four aircraft produced in the initial order of 184 were simply designated B-25s with no model letter. After self-sealing fuel tanks and some armor protection were added, the next forty aircraft were given the B-25A designation. The remaining 120 aircraft in the order were completed as B-25Bs, and they featured two power operated gun turrets for self defense. Each turret had two .50-caliber machine guns, and both were located in the aft fuselage. The top turret featured a clear dome through which the gunner could aim and fire the weapons, while the lower retractable turret was sighted through a periscope. With the addition of these two turrets, the tail and waist guns were deleted from the B-25B.

On April 18, 1942, sixteen B-25Bs flew from the deck of the aircraft carrier USS HORNET, CV-8, on what

Mitchells assigned to the 5th Air Force attack the Japanese at Dagua with dozens of small parachute bombs on February 3, 1944. The B-25 was well suited to low level attacks, and these small bombs were quite effective against parked aircraft. *(USAFM)*

was to become one of the most daring and famous raids of World War II. Led by then Lt. Col. Jimmy Doolittle, the B-25Bs attacked the Japanese homeland, striking Tokyo and other cities.

By this time, large scale production of the B-25 was underway, and it had been named the Mitchell after the sometimes brash and controversial General William S. "Billy" Mitchell, who had pioneered and developed U. S. Army airpower during its early days of struggle and turmoil. Mitchell had been scoffed and even court-martialed for his determination to convince the U. S. military establishment that the airplane was an important and vital weapon that had to be developed with the highest priority. The Japanese attack on Pearl Harbor was the final and most dramatic proof that his prophecies had been correct.

Large orders for B-25Cs and B-25Ds began rolling off the assembly lines in Inglewood, California, and Kansas City, Missouri, respectively. Completed aircraft were rushed to Europe, Africa, and the Pacific, and several allied nations also began receiving the Mitchell into their air forces. In Europe, and to some degree in Africa, B-25Bs and Cs served in the conventional roles that would be expected of a medium bomber. But in the Pacific, the geography meant that many targets could not effectively be attacked with standard horizontal bombing raids flown at high and medium altitudes. Targets, often hidden or dispersed in the dense jungle foliage, had to be attacked at tree top level if they were going to be destroyed.

Lt. Col. Paul "Pappy" Gunn realized that the B-25's airframe could easily be adapted for such missions. By comparison, Martin's B-26 Marauder, the other medium bomber then in production for the USAAF, could not as easily or effectively be modified for such a role. As a result, the B-26s were sent to Europe where, after some initial problems, they became a highly effective medium bomber in the traditional sense.

To maximize the Mitchell's effectiveness as a low-level attack aircraft, Lt. Col. Gunn, working with a North American Technical Representative named Jack Fox, began modifying B-25s in the field. The bomb sight was removed from the nose, and fixed .50-caliber machine guns were mounted inside the bombardier's compartment. Pods containing .50-caliber weapons were often "strapped on" to the sides of the forward fuselage. So successful were Gunn's initial efforts that more Mitchells in increasing numbers were sent through a modification center at Townsville, Australia, to be converted into dedicated strafers. Using their machine guns, parafrag bombs, and standard bombs in fast low-level attacks, these aircraft became very successful at destroying Japanese targets throughout the Pacific.

To further optimize the Mitchell's capabilities as a low-level strafer, and to make it particularly lethal against coastal shipping, submarines, and small warships, a single B-25C was converted to the XB-25G prototype. The entire bombardier's nose was removed, and a shorter solid nose section was installed. In it were two .50-caliber machine guns and a 75-mm cannon. Five service test B-25Gs were also converted from existing B-25Cs. The B-25C contract was then modified so that the final four hundred aircraft could be delivered as B-25Gs, and sixty-three existing B-25Cs were also converted to B-25G standards.

Meanwhile, North American had produced one XB-

B-25Ds of the 77th Bomb Squadron await their crews in the snow at Shemya Army Air Field on Attu, Alaska. The photograph is dated December 1944. (USAFM)

25E, serial number 42-32281, which was used to evaluate an anti-icing system that used engine exhaust gasses. Although the system was successful, no B-25Es were produced. The XB-25F was also a single aircraft developed to study an electrical anti-icing system, but once again no production B-25Fs were ordered.

A proposed high altitude version of the B-25, designated the XB-28, was also ordered. It featured a fuselage with a circular cross section that contained pressurized compartments for its crew members. It was powered by two Pratt & Whitney R-2800-11 engines, each capable of producing 2,000 horsepower. One aircraft was ordered on February 12, 1940, and it first flew on April 24, 1942. This was followed by an XB-28A which flew a year later, but the B-28 was never put into production. By then, the USAAF had decided that its heavy bombers could handle all of the high altitude missions.

Mitchells were also very effective in the anti-shipping role. Ships the size of this Japanese destroyer escort were sometimes cut in half by the B-25's concentrated firepower to the front. (USAFM)

The B-25G and the B-25H had shorter solid noses in place of the standard bombardier's nose. A 75-mm cannon was mounted in the lower left side of the nose to augment the forward firepower of the machine guns. The B-25G, as shown here, also had two .50-caliber machine guns in its nose in addition to the 75-mm cannon. Strap-on gun packs on each side of the forward fuselage could add four more machine guns to the firepower. (USAFM)

Beginning with the B-25H, the top turret was moved forward to a location just aft of the cockpit. During strafing runs, the turret's two machine guns could be used to augment the fire of the fixed armament. The B-25H also had four .50-caliber machine guns in its nose instead of only two as found in the B-25G. The strap-on gun packs are visible on the side of the forward fuselage. (Jones collection)

One major criticism of the B-25 was its lack of defensive firepower. The lower turret had proven ineffective, and it had been deleted during production of the B-25G. The top turret alone was insufficient to provide adequate defensive fire. Various waist and tail gun installations had been added at depots and in the field, but these also left much to be desired. Correcting this problem was finally addressed on the production line with the B-25H. This was another dedicated strafer version of the Mitchell, and like the B-25G, it had a 75-mm cannon in the nose. Fixed machine gun armament in the solid nose was increased from two to four weapons. To correct the problem of insufficient defensive armament, the top turret was moved forward to the navigator's compartment just aft of the cockpit. This left the radio operator's compartment in the rear fuselage section open for the installation of staggered waist gun positions. To make room for a power operated tail turret, the depth of the aft fuselage was increased by seven inches, and a turret with two guns was installed. The gunner was seated under a small greenhouse which provided good visibility for his field of fire.

This same defensive armament arrangement was also installed in the B-25J, which was the final production variant. Although most were produced with the standard bombardier's nose section, some were fitted with a solid nose containing eight .50-caliber machine guns. Like many B-25Cs and B-25Ds before them, B-25Js with the standard nose were often converted for the strafing mission with the addition of extra .50-caliber machine guns. These modified aircraft, along with those fitted with the solid gun nose, continued their effective work as strafers throughout the Pacific right up until the end of the war.

Beginning with the B-25B, the U. S. Navy began to acquire Mitchells of each variant except for the B-25G. (Only one B-25G was obtained as a PBJ-1G.) These aircraft were redesignated PBJ-1s with model letter

The final production version of the Mitchell was the B-25J, which was built with the standard bombardier's nose. However, North American also produced alternate solid nose kits which mounted eight .50-caliber machine guns for use in the strafer role. (USAFM)

This B-25J is fitted with the optional solid nose kit which mounted eight .50-caliber machine guns for use in the strafer role. During production of the B-25J, zero-length mounting stubs for 5-inch rockets were added under the wings. *(USAFM)*

designators being added after the 1 to match those used by the USAAF. Most PBJ-1s were operated by the Marines, and many were used for coastal patrols around the United States. Others were sent to the Pacific where they flew missions against shipping and in support of Marines on the ground. They were often fitted with search radars to help them locate targets at night.

Following the war, many B-25s remained in service with the USAAF and later the United States Air Force. Although their use as combat aircraft quickly ended, they provided valuable service as multi-engine pilot trainers, radar trainers for operators, and transports. Others were used as utility aircraft. The last Mitchell was stricken from the USAF registry in 1960, marking the end of nineteen years of service.

During World War II, Mitchells were provided to Australia, Brazil, Canada, China, Great Britain, The Netherlands, and Russia. Argentina, Bolivia, Chile, Columbia, Cuba, the Dominican Republic, Mexico, Peru, Uruguay, and Venezuela all received Mitchells in the postwar years.

The Navy equivalent of the B-25J was the PBJ-1J. Note the radome on the tip of the right wing in the foreground. Over 700 Mitchells of different variants were obtained by the Navy for use as PBJ-1s during World War II, and most were operated by the Marines. *(National Archives)*

MITCHELL VARIANTS
B-25-NA

The first nine production B-25s were built with wings having a constant dihedral from root to tip as shown here. Beginning with the tenth production aircraft, the outer wing panels were mounted with no dihedral in order to improve stability. **(USAFM)**

The first twenty-four aircraft built were simply designated B-25s with no model letter indicated. They are sometimes referred to as B-25-NAs, to be more specific and to avoid confusion with the B-25 designation as it is often applied in general terms to all Mitchells. The NA suffix stood for the North American facility at Inglewood, California, and all later versions of the B-25 built there also had the NA suffix in their full designations. B-25Ds and B-25Js built at North American's Kansas City plant had the NC suffix.

The first nine B-25-NAs were completed with a constant wing dihedral from root to tip, but after flight testing revealed stability problems, the wing panels outboard of the engine nacelles were mounted so that they had no dihedral on the remaining fifteen B-25-NAs. This resulted in a gull wing design that was carried forward on all subsequent versions.

The B-25-NA was designed to carry up to 3,600 pounds of bombs in an internal bomb bay. Defensive armament consisted of a flexible .30-caliber machine gun in the nose that could be mounted in any one of three ball socket mounts, one to the front, and one on each side. Three .30-caliber waist guns were to be manned by the radio operator. One gun was mounted in a window on each side of the aircraft, and the third gun could be fired through a mount in the large window in the top of the fuselage. The final defensive weapon was a single .50-caliber machine gun mounted in a large tail position.

Some of the twenty-four B-25-NAs were used for flight evaluation, while others were assigned to the 17th Bombardment Group for service tests. The first B-25-

The first production B-25 was flown with a number of different designs for the vertical tails, but it is most often pictured with these smaller tails that had less area than those on all subsequent Mitchells. This aircraft could be identified by its natural metal finish and red, white, and blue stripes on the rudders. **(USAFM)**

One of the first nine B-25-NAs is painted in the standard Olive Drab over Neutral Gray camouflage scheme, and it has the larger vertical tails that became standard on all subsequent Mitchells. However, the wings still retain the constant dihedral from root to tip. *(USAFM)*

NA, serial number 40-2165, was fitted with several different vertical tails, some larger and some smaller than what would become the production standard. Once the best design was chosen, it remained the same for all subsequent versions of the aircraft.

B-25-NAs were powered by two Wright R-2600-9 Cyclone, twin-row, fourteen cylinder, radial engines. These powerplants produced 1,700 horsepower for take-off, and they sustained 1,350 horsepower at 13,000 feet. Although the R-2600 had improvements made to it

Because of the dihedral in the outer wing panels on this early B-25-NA, this side view looks quite different than others taken of later aircraft. The B-25-NA and B-25A had long exhaust pipes on the outside of both engine nacelles. *(USAFM)*

Beginning with the tenth B-25-NA, the outboard wing panels were mounted with zero degrees of dihedral. This created a gull wing that remained unchanged for all of the remaining production variants. (USAFM)

over the years the B-25 was produced, these horsepower ratings remained the same for all variants.

By the time the tenth B-25-NA rolled off the production line, the design for the Mitchell had been established. For all versions that followed, the design of the

A North American employee demonstrates how the tail gunner would occupy the original tail gun position in the first production B-25. Note that he is in a seated position. (Avery collection via Roeder)

wings, horizontal tail, and vertical tails remained unchanged. Most physical changes that were made to the fuselage involved armament installations, including solid gun noses on the B-25G, B-25H, and some B-25Js. An upper turret was mounted first in the aft fuselage compartment, then it was moved to the navigator's compartment just behind the cockpit on the final two production variants. Different waist and tail gun positions were added at modification centers and field depots, and they finally became production standards on the B-25H and B-25J. Otherwise, except for some relatively minor detail differences, the sound, basic design of the B-25-NA remained unchanged throughout the entire production run.

DATA

Version	B-25 (no suffix letter)
North American Model Number	NA-62
Number Built	24
First Flight	August 19, 1940
Powerplants	Wright R-2600-9
Maximum Horsepower (each)	1,700
Maximum Speed	322 mph @ 15,000 feet
Initial Rate of Climb	2,090 feet per minute
Ceiling	30,000 feet
Maximum Combat Range	2,000 miles*
Empty Weight	16,767 pounds
Maximum Take-off Weight	27,310 pounds

* With 916 gallons of fuel and a 3,000-pound bomb load. Range figures varied considerably depending on amount of fuel carried and payload.

B-25-NA, 1/120th SCALE, MULTI-VIEW DRAWINGS

DETAIL & SCALE, COPYRIGHT, MULTI-VIEW DRAWINGS

BY LLOYD S. JONES

DETAIL & SCALE, INC.

1

1/120th SCALE

● MULTI-VIEW DRAWING

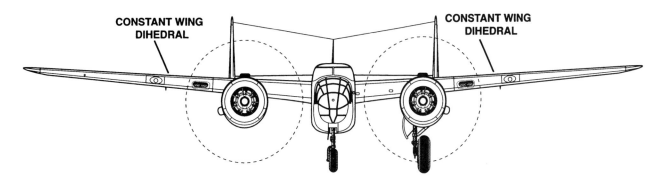

CONSTANT WING DIHEDRAL

CONSTANT WING DIHEDRAL

This front view is for the first nine B-25-NAs with the constant wing dihedral from root to tip.

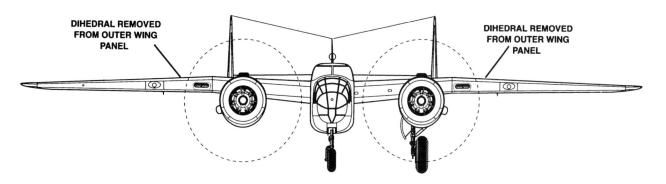

DIHEDRAL REMOVED FROM OUTER WING PANEL

DIHEDRAL REMOVED FROM OUTER WING PANEL

Beginning with the tenth B-25-NA, the outer wing panels had no dihedral angle.

FIRST PRODUCTION B-25

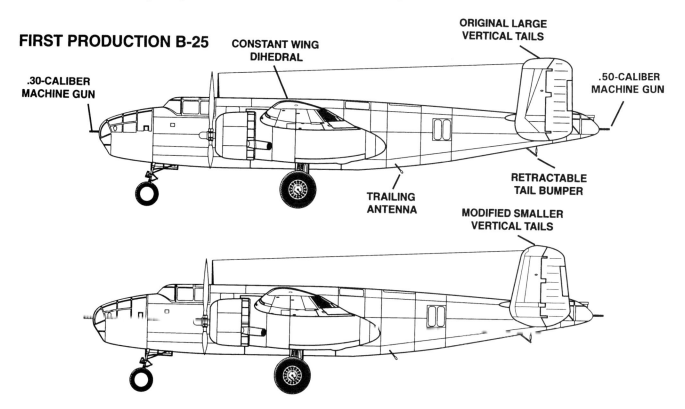

.30-CALIBER MACHINE GUN

CONSTANT WING DIHEDRAL

ORIGINAL LARGE VERTICAL TAILS

.50-CALIBER MACHINE GUN

TRAILING ANTENNA

RETRACTABLE TAIL BUMPER

MODIFIED SMALLER VERTICAL TAILS

13

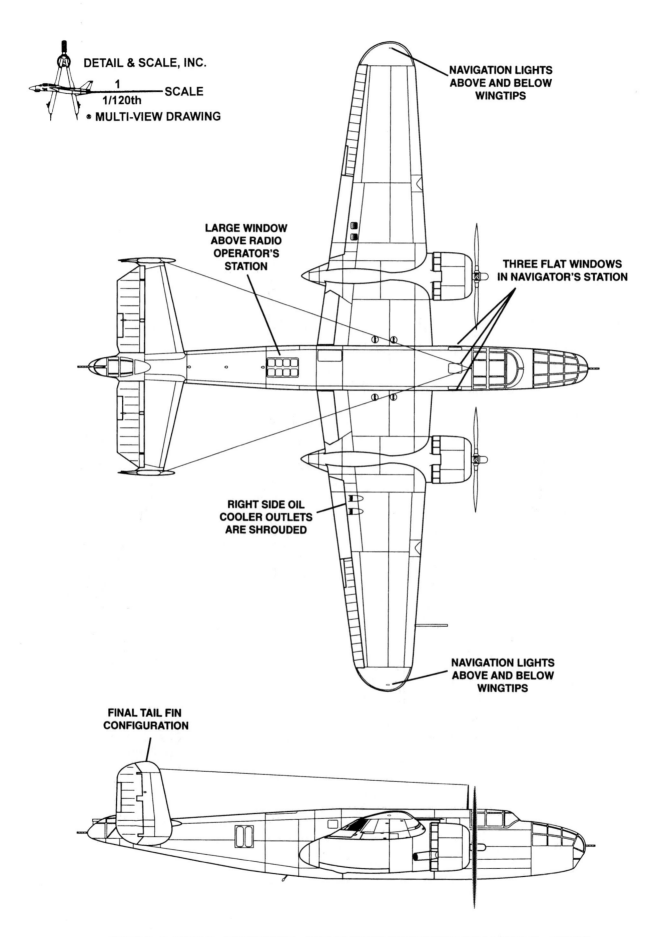

DETAIL & SCALE, INC.

SCALE

1/120th

● MULTI-VIEW DRAWING

NAVIGATION LIGHTS
ABOVE AND BELOW
WINGTIPS

LARGE WINDOW
ABOVE RADIO
OPERATOR'S
STATION

THREE FLAT WINDOWS
IN NAVIGATOR'S STATION

RIGHT SIDE OIL
COOLER OUTLETS
ARE SHROUDED

NAVIGATION LIGHTS
ABOVE AND BELOW
WINGTIPS

FINAL TAIL FIN
CONFIGURATION

DETAIL & SCALE, COPYRIGHT, MULTI-VIEW DRAWINGS BY LLOYD S. JONES

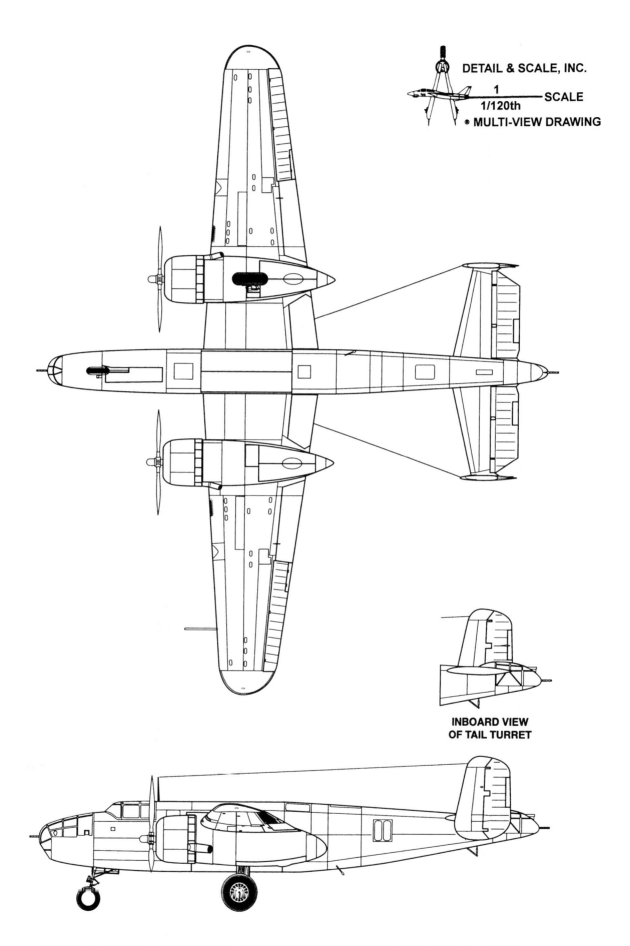

INBOARD VIEW
OF TAIL TURRET

DETAIL & SCALE, COPYRIGHT, MULTI-VIEW DRAWINGS BY LLOYD S. JONES

B-25A

The B-25-NA and B-25A had long exhaust pipes on both engine nacelles. The small circular items in the glass panels of the nose section are mounting sockets for the bombardier's .30-caliber machine gun. Many Mitchells, up through early production B-25Cs and B-25Ds, had ball socket mounts for the machine gun on each side of the nose so that the bombardier could counter aircraft attacking from either side. (USAFM)

Following the twenty-four B-25-NAs, forty B-25As were produced. Externally, these aircraft were identical in appearance to the last fifteen B-25-NAs which had the outer wing panels mounted with no angle of dihedral. Internally, the B-25A had armor plating in back of the seats for the pilot, co-pilot, and bombardier. Armor was also added in the gunner's compartment. Self-sealing fuel tanks were installed, but their capacity was only 694 gallons as compared to 913 gallons in the B-25-NA. As a result, the range of the aircraft suffered considerably.

Depending on the load the aircraft was carrying, combat range was reduced approximately 650 miles. To make up for the loss of fuel capacity in the wings, a droppable tank with a capacity of 418 gallons was designed to be carried in the bomb bay on ferry flights or patrol missions. With the addition of the self-sealing fuel tanks and even a relatively small amount of armor protection, the B-25A was the first version of the Mitchell to be officially considered operationally ready for combat.

Fifteen B-25As soon joined the B-25-NAs already assigned to the 17th Bombardment Group for service tests. Enthusiasm for the new bomber was high as the unit began its transition from the Douglas B-18 Bolo. Six

The B-25A had twin waist windows on the aft side of the fuselage. A top window was also located above the aft fuselage, and three small windows were provided for the navigator's compartment just aft of the cockpit. All three were flush with the skin of the fuselage. (USAFM)

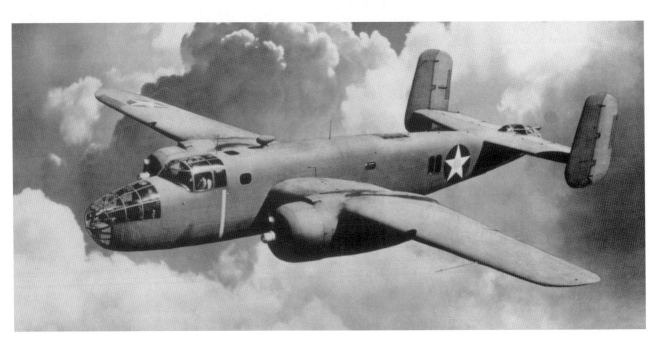

This B-25A was assigned to the 34th Bombardment Squadron of the 17th Bombardment Group and was photographed at Felts Field, Washington, on August 29, 1941. The 17th BG was the first group to become fully operational in Mitchells, and they conducted service tests with the B-25A. *(USAFM)*

each were also sent to the 30th, 39th, 43rd, and 44th Bombardment Groups. One was assigned to Wright Field, Ohio.

By the time the United States entered the war, the B-25B with its powered operated turrets was available, so none of the B-25-NAs or B-25As were sent to combat overseas. Instead, they were used to fly coastal patrols looking for enemy submarines, a mission that did not require the additional defensive armament. For this role, the aircraft were fitted with the extra fuel tank in the bomb bay, and racks for bombs and depth charges were added under the wings. While flying these missions, the B-25 became the first bomber to sink an Axis submarine in the Atlantic. As it was moved around the country from base to base, the 17th Bombardment Squadron flew missions over the Pacific and Atlantic Oceans as well as the Gulf of Mexico. They were also credited with sinking an enemy submarine off both coasts.

DATA

Version	B-25A
North American Model Number	NA-62A
Number Built	40
First Flight	February 25, 1941
Powerplants	Wright R-2600-9
Maximum Horsepower (each)	1,700
Maximum Speed	315 mph @ 15,000 feet
Initial Rate of Climb	1,785 feet per minute
Ceiling	27,000 feet
Maximum Combat Range	1,350 miles*
Empty Weight	17,870 pounds
Maximum Take-off Weight	27,100 pounds

* With 694 gallons of fuel and a 3,000-pound bomb load. Range figures varied considerably depending on the amount of fuel carried and payload.

A .30-caliber machine gun was located inside each of the waist windows. Brackets for ammunition boxes can be seen to the left. *(Avery collection via Roeder)*

Unlike the North American employee shown on page 12, this gunner in a B-25A assumes the prone position to fire the tail gun. *(Rockwell)*

B-25-NA & B-25A DIMENSION DRAWINGS

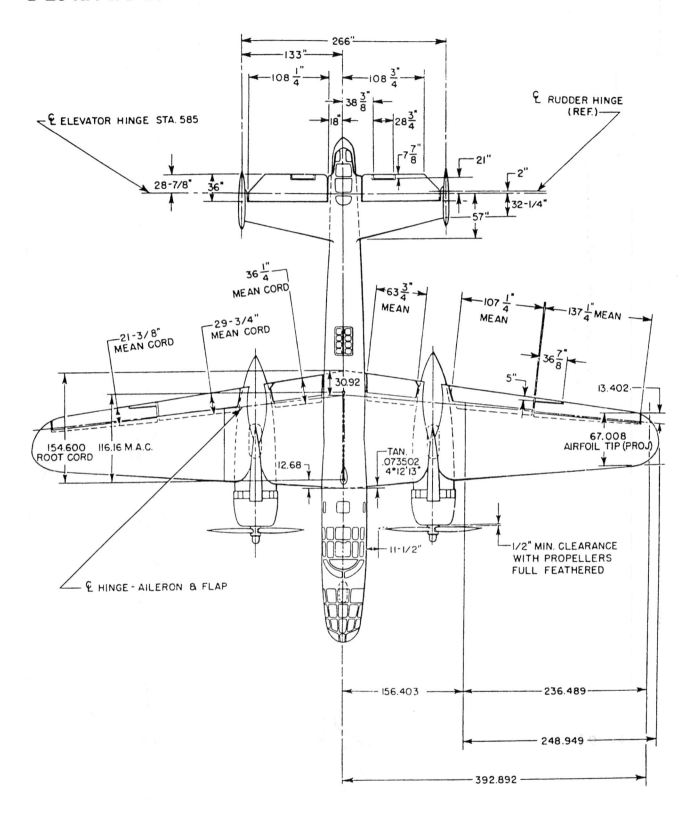

The drawings on this page and the next were taken from the official manual for the B-25, and they indicate the dimensions for both the B-25-NA and the B-25A. Most basic airframe dimensions remained the same for all variants of the Mitchell. *(USAFM)*

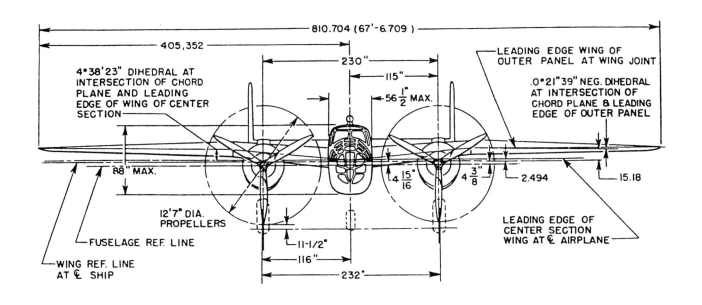

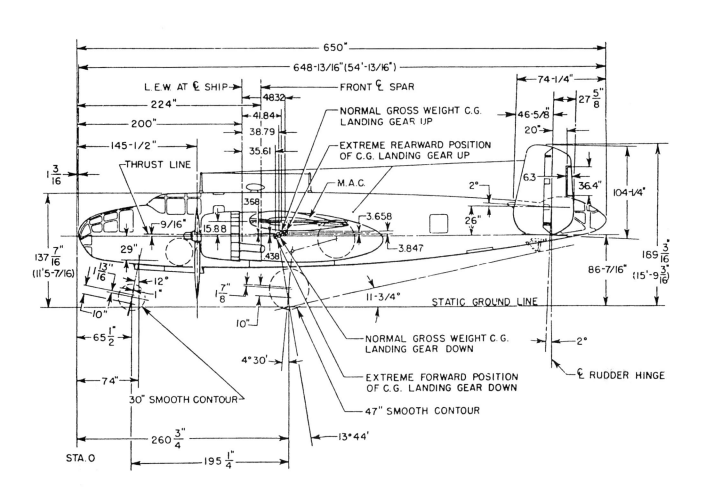

B-25B

From this angle, the most noticeable physical difference between the B-25B and the earlier B-25A was the addition of the top turret mounted aft on the fuselage. The bulge for the retractable lower turret can also be seen beyond the lower propeller blade. The B-25B had a long exhaust pipe on the left nacelle like that used on both nacelles on the B-25 and B-25A. However, the right nacelle had a short stub exhaust. The longer pipe on the left nacelle was necessitated by the presence of a heat exchanger. (USAFM)

Even before the first B-25 was completed, the war in Europe had begun, and Japan was fighting on the Asian continent. Although the United States was not yet directly involved, it was studying the lessons learned and applying them to its new weapons which were then under development. The self-sealing fuel tanks and armor protection, already added to the B-25A, were examples of improvements made as the result of what was happening on the battlefields in Europe and Asia.

It became very evident that light machine guns in single positions were no longer sufficient as defensive armament for bombers. Power operated turrets, usually with two .50-caliber weapons, were developed, and for the Mitchell, these first appeared on the B-25B. With twenty-four B-25-NAs and forty B-25As already delivered, 120 aircraft remained on the initial order for B-25s

approved on September 20, 1939. These 120 aircraft were completed to B-25B standards, however one of them crashed before delivery and was not counted in official totals.

With the installation of the two turrets, the tail gun position and the waist guns were deleted. The large, two-piece, windows, used as firing positions for the waist guns on the B-25-NA and B-25A, were replaced with smaller single windows in the aft fuselage. The elimination of the waist and tail gun positions would subsequently be recognized as a mistake, and some B-25Cs, Ds, and Gs would have waist and tail guns added at modification depots and by units in the field. These would be installed in several different configurations. Finally, both waist and tail gun positions would be restored as production standards on the B-25H and B-25J.

The top turret, added in the B-25B's radio compartment, took the place of the large window fitted in the top of the fuselage on the B-25-NA and B-25A. It was a Bendix design with a clear dome and a gun sight mounted between the two .50-caliber machine guns. It

It was believed that the addition of the two power-operated turrets eliminated the necessity for the two waist guns and the tail gun position. The B-25B therefore had smaller waist windows than the B-25A, and usually there were no guns installed in them. (National Archives)

The top scanning window for the navigator's station, the ADF "football" antenna, and the manned turret are all visible on the top of this B-25B's fuselage. Also note the two small covers over the exhaust vents for the oil cooler ducts on top of the right wing. These were not present on the left wing. **(National Archives)**

was powered operated in azimuth and elevation by an electric motor, and 400 rounds were provided for each gun.

The lower turret was a solid retractable design, and it was sighted through a periscope. Like the top turret, it also had two .50-caliber machine guns, and 350 rounds of ammunition were carried for each. For a number of reasons, this turret was never considered to be very effective. Using the periscope made many crewmen airsick, and even when retracted, dirt, mud, and oil often covered the lens of the periscope. In spite of the fact that additional and larger sighting windows were added in the radio compartment, acquiring targets often proved far more difficult than with a turret having a clear dome. Another problem was that the retraction microswitch could be damaged if the turret was lowered too fast. If this happened, the turret would jam in the down position. This would increase drag and reduce the speed of the aircraft. The lower turret remained a standard feature on B-25Cs and B-25Ds, but it was finally deleted during B-25G production. It was also removed in the field by some units. Radomes replaced the lower turret on some PBJ-1s used by the Navy and Marines.

A minor change on the exterior of the B-25B was that the exhaust pipe on the right engine was changed to a short stub, while the pipe on the left nacelle remained the same longer length used on the B-25-NA and B-25A. The retention of the longer pipe on the left side was due to the presence of a heat exchanger.

When the Japanese attacked Pearl Harbor on December 7, 1941, North American was in the middle of B-25B

production. Some had already been delivered to the 17th Bombardment Group and were serving along side that unit's B-25-NAs and B-25As. It would be aircraft and crews chosen from this unit that would fly the famous Doolittle raid on April 18, 1942, using sixteen B-25Bs.

Approximately two dozen B-25Bs became the first Mitchells to be acquired by the U. S. Navy, and they were redesignated PBJ-1Bs. These aircraft were used by the Marines for coastal patrols, and by war's end, over seven hundred PBJ-1s of all variants would be delivered to the Navy. The Royal Air Force received twenty-three B-25Bs which it named the Mitchell I, and two were delivered to Russia. Both of these nations would subsequently receive many more Mitchells during the war.

DATA

Version	B-25B
North American Model Number	NA-62B
U. S. Navy/Marine Designation	PBJ-1B
British Designation	Mitchell I
Number Built	120*
First Delivery	August 1941
Last Delivery	January 1942
Powerplants	Wright R-2600-9
Maximum Horsepower (each)	1,700
Maximum Speed	300 mph @ 15,000 feet
Initial Rate of Climb	1,704 feet per minute
Ceiling	23,500 feet
Maximum Range	1,300 miles**
Empty Weight	20,000 pounds
Maximum Take-off Weight	28,460 pounds

* The fifteenth B-25B, 40-2243, crashed before delivery, so only 119 were delivered.
** With 694 gallons of fuel and a 3,000-pound bomb load. Range figures varied considerably depending on the amount of fuel carried and payload.

B-25B DETAILS

The large tail gun position of the B-25 and the B-25A was replaced with a more tapered tail ending in a clear blister on the B-25B. This remained a production standard for the B-25C, D, and G, although some of these aircraft had tail guns added at depots or in the field.

(National Archives)

Jimmy Doolittle installed two broomsticks in the tail dome of his B-25B to discourage attacks from the rear. Photographs of the raiders prove that at least some of the other crews did the same. Black paint has been applied to the clear dome on this B-25B to simulate slots for the gun barrels. *(National Archives)*

Center left and right: The manned Bendix top turret was mounted under a clear dome, and the gunner lined up his targets through a sight located between the weapons. At left is a view of the turret as seen from the left side of the aircraft. At right is a look at the turret's details with the clear dome removed. *(Both National Archives)*

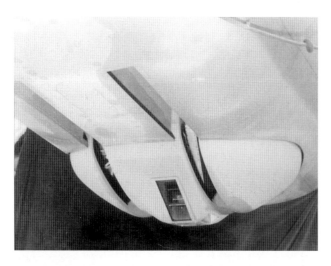

The Bendix lower turret was a solid remote controlled design, and it could be aimed through a periscopic sight. The turret is shown here in the retracted position, and the gun barrels are up inside the two rectangular slots. This view looks forward from beneath the aft fuselage.

(Avery collection via Roeder)

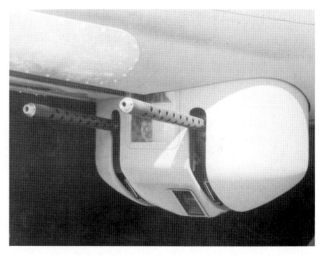

Here the lower turret is fully extended and ready to fire. It proved difficult to use, and visibility was very restricted even with the addition of scanning windows in the radio operator's position. The lower turret was retained on the B-25C and B-25D, but it was deleted during B-25G production. *(Avery collection via Roeder)*

The cockpit of the B-25B was very typical for the late 1930s and early 1940s, with identical control columns provided for both the pilot and co-pilot. Engine and propeller controls were on a pedestal between the two yokes. (Avery collection via Roeder)

Details on the left side of the cockpit are revealed in this view. Cockpit surfaces were painted Chromate Green Primer, while the instrument panel and control yokes were flat black. The grips on the yokes were silver. (Avery collection via Roeder)

B-25B, 1/120th SCALE, MULTI-VIEW DRAWINGS

DETAIL & SCALE, INC.

1
———— SCALE
1/120th

• MULTI-VIEW DRAWING

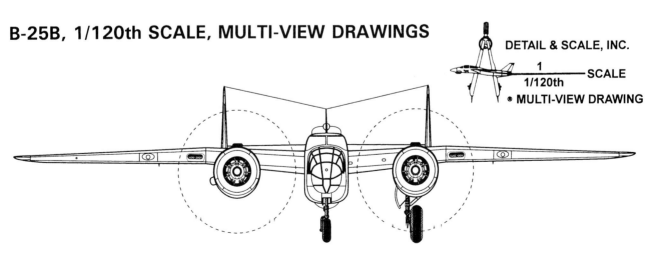

DETAIL & SCALE, COPYRIGHT, MULTI-VIEW DRAWINGS BY LLOYD S. JONES

DETAIL & SCALE, INC.

1 ──── SCALE

1/120th

⊛ MULTI-VIEW DRAWING

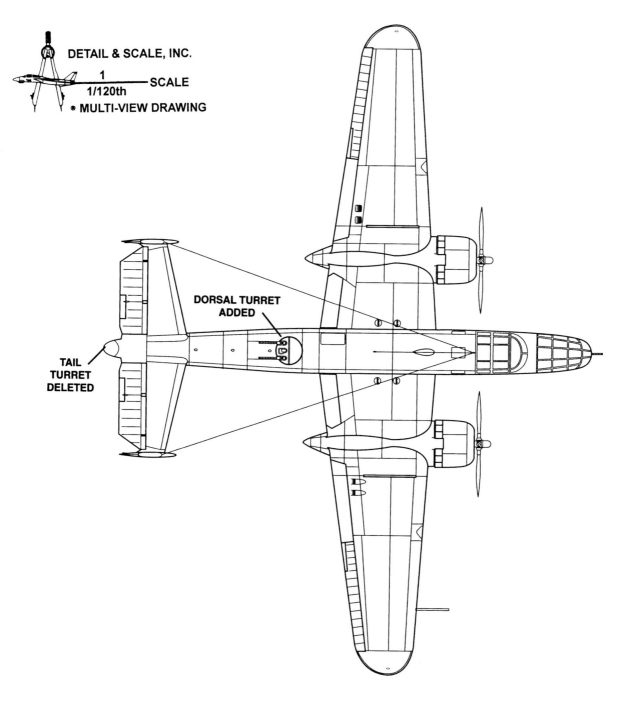

DORSAL TURRET ADDED

TAIL TURRET DELETED

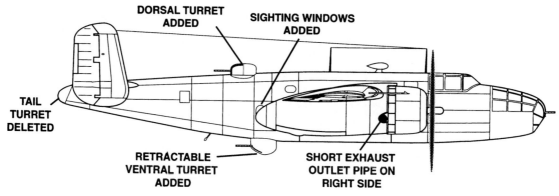

DORSAL TURRET ADDED

SIGHTING WINDOWS ADDED

TAIL TURRET DELETED

RETRACTABLE VENTRAL TURRET ADDED

SHORT EXHAUST OUTLET PIPE ON RIGHT SIDE

DETAIL & SCALE, COPYRIGHT, MULTI-VIEW DRAWINGS BY LLOYD S. JONES

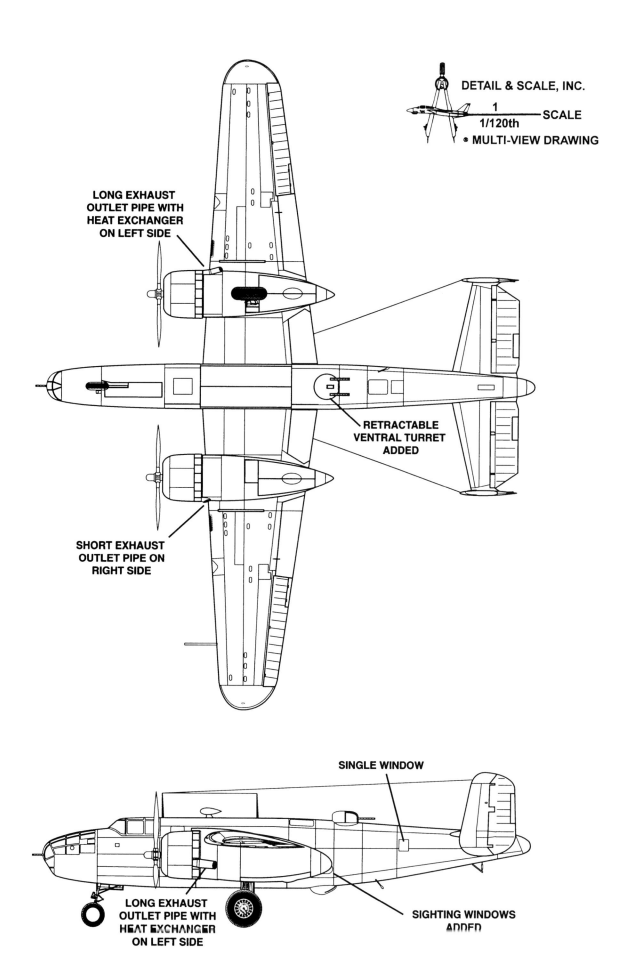

DETAIL & SCALE, INC.

1 — SCALE
1/120th

⊕ MULTI-VIEW DRAWING

LONG EXHAUST
OUTLET PIPE WITH
HEAT EXCHANGER
ON LEFT SIDE

SHORT EXHAUST
OUTLET PIPE ON
RIGHT SIDE

RETRACTABLE
VENTRAL TURRET
ADDED

SINGLE WINDOW

LONG EXHAUST
OUTLET PIPE WITH
HEAT EXCHANGER
ON LEFT SIDE

SIGHTING WINDOWS
ADDED

DETAIL & SCALE, COPYRIGHT, MULTI-VIEW DRAWINGS BY LLOYD S. JONES

B-25C

The B-25C was the first version of the Mitchell to be built in large numbers. This early B-25C-NA, 41-12800, has the flat windows in the navigator's compartment and the smooth cowlings as used on the earlier variants.
(National Archives)

The production of B-25-NAs, B-25As, and B-25Bs combined totalled only 184 aircraft, and of these, 183 were delivered. The B-25C was the first version built in large numbers, because by the time deliveries to the Army began in January 1942, America had become involved in the war. Orders for all military equipment had increased to levels many times that of prewar production. The number of B-25Cs that would be built at North American's Inglewood, California, plant would eventually total 1,625 aircraft. While these were being built, a second line was opened at Kansas City, Missouri, to produce 2,290 B-25Ds which were essentially the same as the B-25C. By this time, the aircraft had been officially named the Mitchell in honor of General Billy Mitchell who was a major pioneer in the development of airpower within the U. S. Army.

When the first B-25C rolled off the production line, it looked very much like the previous B-25B. The R-2600-13 version of the Wright Cyclone engine had replaced the R-2600-9 used on the earlier Mitchell variants, but, contrary to what has been stated in another reference, the R-2600-13 did not offer any additional horsepower. The difference between the two versions of the engine was that the R-2600-13 was fitted with Holley carburetors instead of Bendix Stromberg units as used on the R-2600-9. These carburetors were also equipped with air filtering units. Fuel vents were added at the aft end of

each nacelle, and a 24-volt electrical system was installed. The retractable tail skid was replaced with a fixed fairing under the aft fuselage.

Other improvements fitted to all B-25Cs included a Stewart Warner cabin heater, remote indicating Autosyne instruments, and a high pressure brake system that replaced the low pressure system on the earlier aircraft. An emergency hydraulic landing gear extension system was added in the event of a failure of the main system. The bomb racks inside the bomb bay were redesigned and equipped with A-2 electrical releases.

A number of other important improvements and changes were made to this version of the Mitchell, and most references also attribute them to all aircraft in the B-25C production blocks. But this simply was not the case. These changes and improvements were made over the course of the production run, and the most important of them are summarized here in the order in which they occurred. However, it should be noted that some of these changes were retrofitted to earlier aircraft at times.

Beginning with B-25C-NA, 41-12817, the fuel capacity was increased to 974 gallons. An astrodome replaced the flat scanning window in the top of the fuselage above the navigator's compartment, although photographic evidence would indicate that some aircraft after this one had the flat window installed. The gun turrets were changed to the Bendix Amplidine type.

B-25C-1-NA, 41-13039, was the first Mitchell to have provisions for under-wing bomb racks installed as a production standard. The outer wing structure was strengthened as well. The capability to carry and launch a 2,000-pound torpedo on a rack beneath the bomb bay was also added at this time.

Several major changes took place beginning with B-

The retracted lower turret is visible in this underside view. Also note the fixed tail bumper in the form of a fairing beneath the aft fuselage. This feature first appeared on the B-25C and remained standard on all future Mitchell variants. B-25Cs and B-25Ds had short exhaust stubs on both engine nacelles. **(National Archives)**

25C-5-NA, 42-53332. The .30-caliber flexible gun was replaced by a .50-caliber weapon and metal framework was added around the ball socket on the front of the nose to handle the increased weight of the larger gun. The two ball sockets for mounting the gun on the sides of the nose were deleted. A fixed .50-caliber machine gun was also added in the nose on the right side, and it was fired by the pilot. Winterization equipment was added, but the deicing boots on the wings and tail surfaces were often deleted in climates where icing was not likely to be a problem. B-25Cs starting with 42-53332 had a "finger" style flame dampening exhaust collector.

Starting with B-25C-10-NA, 42-32233, a remote reading compass was added, and additional cabin heating provisions were installed. The flat scanning windows on each side of the navigator's compartment were changed to a blistered design.

Clayton "S" type flame dampening stacks were first installed on B-25C-15-NA, 42-32383. These stacks were fitted individually to all fourteen cylinders rather than routing the exhaust to a single collector on each side. Each stack was covered by a small fairing on the outside of the cowling.

On B-25C-25-NA, 42-64702, and subsequent C models, the windshield framework was modified to what was called a "clear vision" style. The capability was added to carry a 230-gallon, self-sealing, fuel cell in the bomb bay. As an option, provisions for a 325-gallon metal fuel tank were installed in the bomb bay on every second aircraft.

The need for additional defensive armament was immediately recognized, and some B-25Cs had tail and/or waist guns added at modification centers or by units in the field. In some cases, .30-caliber weapons were mounted in the existing small windows on each side of the aft fuselage, while on other aircraft, larger windows for .50-caliber machine guns were cut into the fuselage near the trailing edge of the wing. These would sometimes be fitted with sliding panels to cover the windows when the guns were not being employed.

To provide additional protection from stern attacks, the clear dome was sometimes removed from the tail, and a single .30 or .50-caliber weapon was mounted in the opening. The gunner had to lie down on a mat to fire the weapon, and his field of vision and fire was quite limited. In a few cases, a tail gun position was added that looked something like the installation that would later appear on the B-25H and B-25J, but it was smaller and had only a single .50-caliber machine gun.

Some interesting changes were made to the armament in the nose of some B-25Cs sent to the Pacific where low level strafing attacks were more effective than the standard horizontal bombing runs usually associated with medium and heavy bombers. Lt. Col. Jack "Pappy"

These early B-25C-NAs were assigned to the 3rd Bomb Group in April 1942. *(USAFM)*

Gunn began having B-25Cs and B-25Ds modified to improve their capabilities as strafers. The bomb sight was removed from the nose section, and additional .50-caliber machine guns were installed in fixed mounts. About this time, strap-on gun packs also began to appear on the forward fuselage sides. The idea was to bring as many heavy machine guns as possible to bear on the target as the Mitchell made a strafing pass at low level. Parafrag bombs were also dropped from low altitudes against aircraft and other targets, and these were the forerunners of today's high drag air inflatable retard (AIR) bombs. Many B-25Cs and B-25Ds that were modified for the strafer role also had the rear dome removed and the single .30 or .50-caliber machine gun added in the tail.

Some B-25Cs were used for training and designated AT-24Cs. This was later changed to TB-25C after the war in June 1948. The Navy acquired 60 B-25Cs which it redesignated PBJ-1Cs, while Great Britain, The Netherlands, France, Australia, and China all received B-25Cs during the war as well. The Royal Air Force called both its B-25Cs and B-25Ds Mitchell IIs.

DATA

Version	B-25C
North American Model Numbers	NA-82, NA-90, NA-93, NA-94, NA-96
U. S. Navy/Marine Designation	PBJ-1C*
British Designation	Mitchell II
Number Built	1,625
First Flight	November 9, 1941
First Delivery	January 1942
Last Delivery	May 1943
Powerplants	Wright R-2600-13
Maximum Horsepower (each)	1,700
Maximum Speed	284 mph @ 15,000 feet
Initial Rate of Climb	1,375 feet per minute
Ceiling	21,200 feet
Maximum Combat Range	1,525 miles***
Empty Weight	20,300 pounds
Maximum Take-off Weight	33,500 pounds

* 60 PBJ-1Cs were acquired by the USN Bureau of Aeronautics.
** With 974 gallons of fuel and a 3,200-pound bomb load. Range figures varied considerably depending on the amount of fuel carried and payload.

This well known photograph shows the proximity of the pilot and co-pilot in the cockpit of a B-25C. Details were almost identical to that in the B-25B. *(Jones collection)*

The right main landing gear on B-25C-NA, 41-12898, collapsed on landing at Port Morsby. This Mitchell was assigned to the 38th Bomb Group. *(USAFM)*

During the B-25C production run, the two side windows for the navigator's compartment were blistered slightly to improve visibility. The flat top window (not visible in this photograph) was replaced with an astrodome. (USAFM)

Some B-25Cs were modified to be used in the strafer role. The bomb sight was removed, and additional .50-caliber machine guns were added in the nose compartment. Although the standard bombardier's nose remained in place, it was often painted over with art as in this case on "DIRTY DORA." (Piet collection)

A few B-25Cs and B-25Ds also had their tail domes removed, and a single .50-caliber machine gun was added. The gunner had to lie down on a mat and use a pillow to fire the gun through the small opening. The visibility and field of fire was very limited. The Marines also installed this gun on some PBJ-1Cs and PBJ-1Ds.
(National Archives)

When wartime experience indicated that additional defensive armament was required, some B-25Cs and B-25Ds had waist guns added at modification centers or in the field. This B-25C has .50-caliber machine guns added in waist windows that have sliding covers installed over them. (Rockwell)

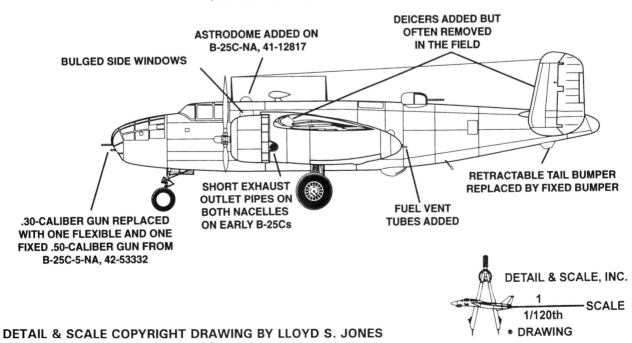

DEICERS ADDED BUT OFTEN REMOVED IN THE FIELD

ASTRODOME ADDED ON B-25C-NA, 41-12817

BULGED SIDE WINDOWS

.30-CALIBER GUN REPLACED WITH ONE FLEXIBLE AND ONE FIXED .50-CALIBER GUN FROM B-25C-5-NA, 42-53332

SHORT EXHAUST OUTLET PIPES ON BOTH NACELLES ON EARLY B-25Cs

FUEL VENT TUBES ADDED

RETRACTABLE TAIL BUMPER REPLACED BY FIXED BUMPER

DETAIL & SCALE, INC.

1
1/120th
SCALE
• DRAWING

DETAIL & SCALE COPYRIGHT DRAWING BY LLOYD S. JONES

B-25D & F-10

B-25D-NC, 41-29651, was the fourth D-model built, and it is shown here at Kansas City. It has been modified with large windows in the radio operator's compartment so that .50-caliber machine guns could be installed in the waist. Note that this early B-25D has the smooth cowlings as found on the B-25B. **(National Archives)**

After the United States entered World War II, North American's plant at Inglewood, California, was not able to produce all of the Mitchells that were required to meet wartime demands, so a second assembly line was opened in Kansas City, Missouri. The NA manufacturers suffix continued to be applied to aircraft built at Inglewood, while NC was used for those produced in Kansas City. But evidently, the USAAF did not believe this was sufficient enough to differentiate between the two, so in spite of the fact that the plants were producing identical aircraft, different model letters were also assigned. The Mitchells built at Inglewood were designated B-25Cs and those coming off the line in Kansas City were called B-25Ds.

The B-25D had all of the improvements found in the B-25C, including the Wright R-2600-13 powerplants with Holley carburetors. The fuel vents at the aft end of the nacelles and the twenty-four volt electrical systems were installed. The B-25D had the tail bumper fairing that replaced the retractable tail skid found on the earlier variants. They also had the Stewart Warner cabin heater, remote indicating Autosyne instruments, high pressure brake system, and internal bomb racks equipped with the A-2 electrical release.

Other improvements and changes that were introduced during production of the B-25C were also added on the line to B-25Ds, however these did not always occur at the same time with respect to block numbers. A summary of the major changes and when they occurred begins with B-25D-1-NC, 41-29848. Starting with that aircraft, provisions for external under-wing bomb racks were added as a production standard, and the outer wing panels were strengthened. Self-sealing fuel cells in the outboard wing section were added, as were carburetor air filters. The astrodome in the navigators compartment and the "finger" style exhaust collectors were also first installed on that B-25D. Oil tanks were changed to the self-sealing type, and Bendix

Amplidyne turrets became standard.

Beginning with B-25D-5-NC, 41-29948, the flexible machine gun in the nose was changed to a .50-caliber weapon, and the ball socket mounts on the sides of the bombardier's compartment were deleted. The forward socket mount was reinforced with a metal plate to handle the weight of the heavier weapon. A fixed .50-caliber machine gun was also added in the right side of the nose, and the scanning windows were changed to the blistered design. Cabin heating was improved starting with B-25D-5-NC, 41-30057.

More improvements were added in the B-25D-10-NC production block. Starting with the first aircraft in this block, 41-30173, winterization equipment was added, although the deicing boots were often removed from these aircraft in the field. The emergency landing gear extension system was added along with a remote reading compass.

A noticeable physical change began with B-25D-15-NC, 41-30353, when the Clayton "S" type exhaust stacks were added to each cylinder along with the fairings that covered them on the cowlings.

The "clear vision" windshield and the 230-gallon, self-sealing, bomb bay fuel tank were added in production starting with B-25D-20-NC, 41-30533. On every second aircraft, provisions were made for a 325-gallon metal fuel tank in the bomb bay. In the cockpit, armor plate was added behind the co-pilot, and a change was made from the Autosyne to A/N pressure type oil, manifold, and fuel pressure instruments. A D-14 type tachometer was also installed.

A portable oxygen system was first added on B-25D-25-NC, 42-87138, and beginning with B-25D-25-NC, 42-87453, improvements were made to the winterization equipment to include a heated air defrosting panel for the windscreen.

Like the B-25Cs, some B-25Ds had defensive tail and waist gun positions added at modification depots and in the field. At times, .30-caliber machine guns were mounted in the existing small waist windows on each side of the aircraft, but in other cases, larger windows were cut into the fuselage sides near the trailing edge of the wing. More potent .50-caliber guns were mounted in these windows, and they were sometimes protected with sliding covers. A simple tail gun installation involved the removal of the clear dome at the aft end of the fuselage.

Either a .30-caliber or .50-caliber machine gun was then mounted in the opening, but the field of view and fire for the weapon was extremely limited. A more complex modification involved the addition of a small greenhouse for the gunner and a single .50-caliber weapon. Although there is evidence this tail gun installation was added to a few B-25Cs and B-25Ds at depots, it appears to have been used more often on B-25Gs.

Like the B-25Cs, many B-25Ds sent to the Pacific were modified at Townsville, Australia, to optimize their capabilities as strafers. The bomb sights were removed from the nose, and fixed machine guns were added. Gun packs were sometimes added to the sides of the forward fuselage, and it was these aircraft that often had the extra machine guns added in the waist and tail as well.

Forty-five aircraft in the B-25D contract became F-10 photographic reconnaissance aircraft. Four were used by Canada, then they were returned to the USAAF. The F-10 was powered by R-2600-29 engines instead of the R-2600-13s used in the B-25D. The two gun turrets were removed, and three K-17 cameras were added in the nose. One was positioned vertically, while the other two were mounted at oblique angles in blisters on each side of the nose section. Additional cameras could be carried in the aft fuselage as they were on most standard bomber versions of the Mitchell. Although these aircraft could be used for combat reconnaissance, their primary function was that of ground mapping.

The Bureau of Aeronautics acquired 151 B-25Ds which were redesignated PBJ-1Ds. Like some of their B-25D counterparts, many of these had the extra defensive armament added in the waist and tail positions, although it appears that when waist guns were added, they were simply .30-caliber weapons mounted in the existing small windows on each side of the aft fuselage. To increase offensive firepower, dual gun packs were often added to the sides of the forward fuselage, and some PBJ-1Ds had radomes for surface search radars in place of their lower turrets.

Most foreign nations that received B-25Cs also obtained B-25Ds, and the Royal Air Force used the name Mitchell II for both. Australia, China, Canada, France, The Netherlands, and Russia also operated B-25Ds during World War II.

At first, the training version of the B-25D was designated AT-24A, but in the post-war redesignation that took place on June 11, 1948, this was changed to TB-25D. At the same time, the F-10 designation became RB-25D.

DATA

Version	B-25D
North American Model Numbers	NA-87, NA-100
U. S. Navy/Marine Designation	PBJ-1D*
British Designation	Mitchell II
Number Built	2,290**
First Flight	January 3, 1942
First Delivery	February 1942
Last Delivery	March 1944
Powerplants	Wright R-2600-13
Maximum Horsepower (each)	1,700
Maximum Speed	284 mph @ 15,000 feet
Initial Rate of Climb	1,375 feet per minute
Ceiling	21,200 feet
Maximum Combat Range	1,525 miles***
Empty Weight	20,300 pounds
Maximum Take-off Weight	33,500 pounds

* 151 PBJ-1Ds were acquired by the USN Bureau of Aeronautics.

** Forty-five were converted to F-10 photographic reconnaissance aircraft.

*** With 974 gallons of fuel and a 3,200-pound bomb load. Range figures varied considerably depending on the amount of fuel carried and payload.

The F-10 was a photographic reconnaissance version of the B-25D. It had fairings for cameras in the nose, and additional cameras were carried in the aft fuselage. The gun turrets were removed. This F-10 was assigned to the 311th Photo Wing at Buckley Field, Colorado. After the war, F-10s remaining in service were redesignated RB-25Ds. (National Archives)

Some B-25Ds and PBJ-1Ds had a tail gun position added at modification centers. It was similar, but not identical, to the tail gun positions that later appeared on B-25Hs and B-25Js. A tail gun position has been added to this PBJ-1D, but no waist guns have been installed. Dual gun packs have been fitted to the sides of the forward fuselage. Also note the radome in place of the lower turret on this particular aircraft. *(National Archives)*

Details on the instrument panel of a B-25D were very much like those in the B-25B and B-25C. *(USAFM)*

A close-up shows details of the waist gun positions installed in some B-25Cs and B-25Ds at modification depots. This is the same installation as seen in the aircraft on page 30. *(National Archives)*

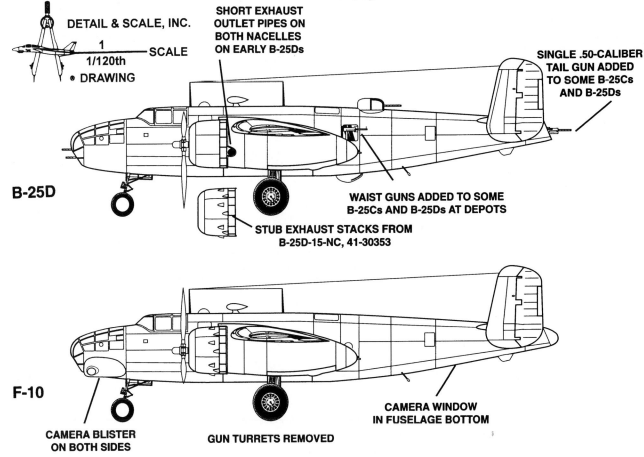

DETAIL & SCALE, INC.

1 ——— SCALE
1/120th
● DRAWING

SHORT EXHAUST OUTLET PIPES ON BOTH NACELLES ON EARLY B-25Ds

SINGLE .50-CALIBER TAIL GUN ADDED TO SOME B-25Cs AND B-25Ds

B-25D

WAIST GUNS ADDED TO SOME B-25Cs AND B-25Ds AT DEPOTS

STUB EXHAUST STACKS FROM B-25D-15-NC, 41-30353

F-10

CAMERA BLISTER ON BOTH SIDES

GUN TURRETS REMOVED

CAMERA WINDOW IN FUSELAGE BOTTOM

DETAIL & SCALE COPYRIGHT DRAWING BY LLOYD S. JONES

B-25 MITCHELL COLORS

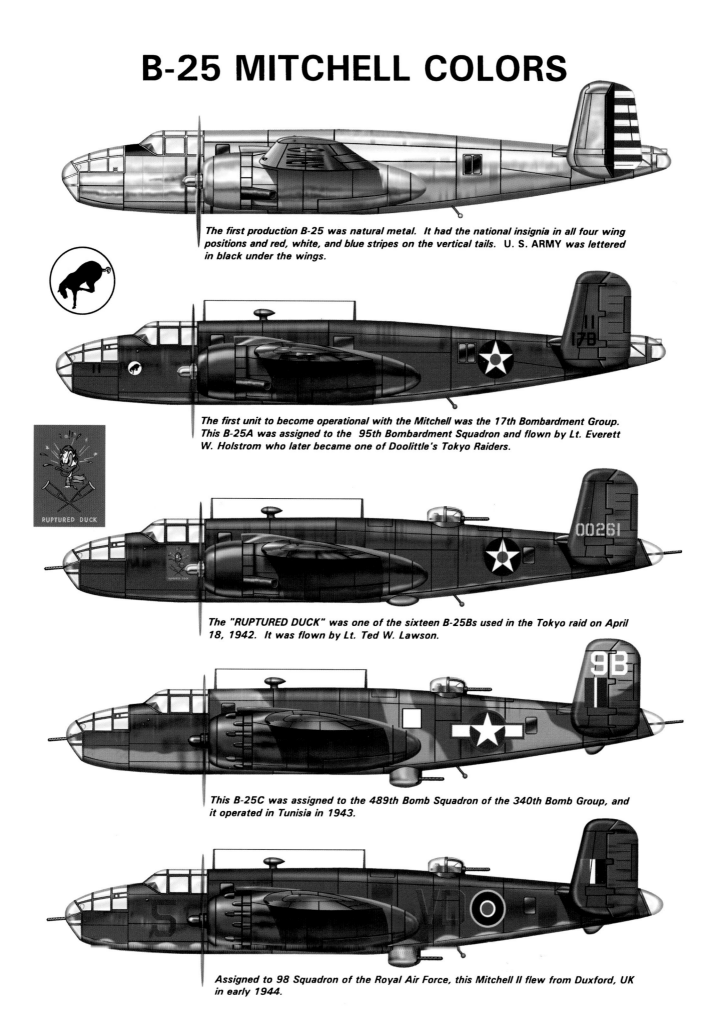

The first production B-25 was natural metal. It had the national insignia in all four wing positions and red, white, and blue stripes on the vertical tails. U. S. ARMY was lettered in black under the wings.

The first unit to become operational with the Mitchell was the 17th Bombardment Group. This B-25A was assigned to the 95th Bombardment Squadron and flown by Lt. Everett W. Holstrom who later became one of Doolittle's Tokyo Raiders.

RUPTURED DUCK

The "RUPTURED DUCK" was one of the sixteen B-25Bs used in the Tokyo raid on April 18, 1942. It was flown by Lt. Ted W. Lawson.

This B-25C was assigned to the 489th Bomb Squadron of the 340th Bomb Group, and it operated in Tunisia in 1943.

Assigned to 98 Squadron of the Royal Air Force, this Mitchell II flew from Duxford, UK in early 1944.

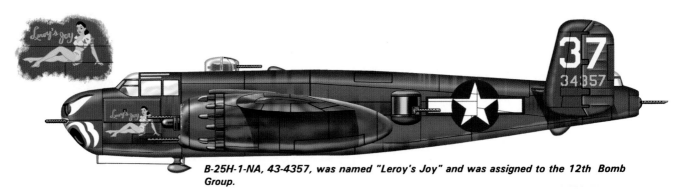

B-25H-1-NA, 43-4357, was named "Leroy's Joy" and was assigned to the 12th Bomb Group.

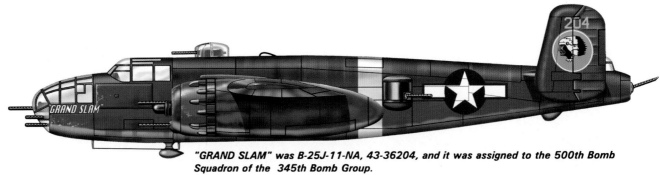

"GRAND SLAM" was B-25J-11-NA, 43-36204, and it was assigned to the 500th Bomb Squadron of the 345th Bomb Group.

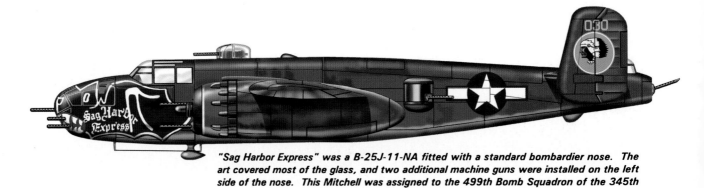

"Sag Harbor Express" was a B-25J-11-NA fitted with a standard bombardier nose. The art covered most of the glass, and two additional machine guns were installed on the left side of the nose. This Mitchell was assigned to the 499th Bomb Squadron of the 345th Bomb Group at Tacloban in the Philippine Islands during January 1945.

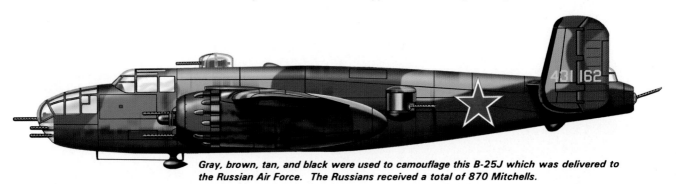

Gray, brown, tan, and black were used to camouflage this B-25J which was delivered to the Russian Air Force. The Russians received a total of 870 Mitchells.

The 405th Bomb Squadron of the 38th Bomb Group operated this B-25J-32-NC which was fitted with the solid gun nose containing eight .50-caliber machine guns. Throughout the war, the 405th BS painted green dragon faces on the noses of its Mitchells.

Above: The Thunderbird insignia of the 17th Bombardment Group's 34th Bombardment Squadron is displayed on the nose of this B-25A. The 17B on the vertical tail indicates the 17th BG, while the 43 on the vertical tail and nose is the aircraft's number within the unit. Note the early style national insignia with the red disc at its center. (via Piet)

Left: By the time B-25Bs were in widespread use, the unit and aircraft numbers on the vertical tail had been replaced with the serial number which was stencilled in yellow. Standard practice was to delete the first digit of the serial number which was 4 for all versions of the B-25. (via Piet)

Right: B-25C-15-NA, 42-32505, is painted in the "desert pink" and Neutral Gray colors common to B-25s and other aircraft serving in Africa. The light tan color was far more suitable for use over the desert than the standard Olive Drab and Neutral Gray scheme seen on the two aircraft above. Often, green splotches or a pattern of green areas would be applied in the field over the tan color to break up the aircraft's outline.

(via Piet)

Above: Although most B-25Ds were camouflaged in one of several different paint schemes, "CHOW HOUND JUNIOR" was a natural metal Mitchell assigned to the 499th Bomb Squadron of the 345th Bomb Group.
(Reinbold via Piet)

Left: This close-up provides a detailed look at the nose art on "CHOW HOUND JUNIOR." (Reinbold via Piet)

Below: The bulged camera fairing on the nose of this Mitchell indicates that it is an F-10 photo reconnaissance version. This picture was taken at Buckley Field, Colorado, in March 1945. (Griffith via Piet)

B-25H & PBJ-1H COLORS

Above: Mitchells of the 12th Bomb Group usually had interesting nose art and names regardless of whether they were camouflaged or natural metal. "Silver Streak" was B-25H-10-NA, 43-4947. (Piet collection)

Right: "EATIN' KITTY" was a camouflaged B-25H assigned to the 63rd BS of the 12th BG. (Piet collection)

Below: This line-up of Marine PBJ-1Hs illustrates how the Navy applied its tri-color paint scheme of Dark Sea Blue, Intermediate Blue, and Flat White to many of its Mitchells. PBJ-1s seldom carried any unit or distinctive markings. (Varga collection via Piet)

B-25J COLORS

Above: These B-25Js have the solid noses with the eight .50-caliber machine guns installed. The black panther nose art indicates that they are assigned to the 501st Bomb Squadron of the 345th Bomb Group.
(Piet collection)

Left: A factory fresh B-25J-25-NC, 44-30004, awaits delivery to the Russian Air Force. It carries its USAAF serial number on the vertical tail in yellow. (Varga collection via Piet)

"OH DEE WHIZZ!" displays numerous mission markings indicating its service with the 63rd Bomb Squadron of the 12th Bomb Group. The nose of this aircraft is fitted with the single flexible .50-caliber machine gun and the two fixed guns on the right side. This arrangement was the production standard for B-25Js fitted with the usual glass bombardier nose. (Piet collection)

Some B-25Js assigned to the 499th BS of the 345th BG had elaborate art painted over the glass portion of their standard bombardier noses. "MY DUCHESS" was one such example. Two additional machine guns were installed in the left side of the nose compartment in an arrangement that mirrored the standard two guns on the right. (Eppstein collection via Piet)

LANDING GEAR DETAILS & COLORS

NOSE LANDING GEAR

Above, left and right: The landing gear remained basically the same on all B-25 variants. The single fork design of the nose gear is illustrated in these two views, however it should be noted that the hydraulic fluid has been removed from this aircraft which is on display at the U. S. Air Force Museum. Therefore, the oleo portion of the gear is fully collapsed. The larger gear door remains in the closed position when the gear is extended, and only the smaller door is open to allow clearance for the strut and drag link.

On this operational aircraft, hydraulic fluid and pressure is present in the nose gear, and the oleo is extended the amount it normally would be when the weight of the aircraft is resting on it. Covers were sometimes fitted over the nose gear wheel. (IPMS Spruce Goose Chapter)

In most cases, the wheels were left uncovered, and the eight spokes were visible. Several different tread designs were used on the tires depending on the conditions in which the aircraft operated. The diamond tread design is shown here.

RIGHT LANDING GEAR

Details on the outside of the right main landing gear are visible here. The wheels, struts, and inside surfaces of the doors were usually painted an aluminum color or were bare metal. The open door in this picture is the right bomb bay door in the background rather than a landing gear door.

The inside of the right main wheel looked much like the outside except where the strut fit into the hub. The oleo link was on the forward side of the strut, and a brake line ran from inside the strut to the connections on the wheel.

When the gear was extended, one small door remained open to provide clearance for the strut. It was operated by a rod which extended between the drag link and the door. The open area forward of the gear is not part of the wheel well, but it is an open access panel on the underside of the nacelle.

In this low front view, the open strut door is shown from a different angle, and additional details of the main strut, link, and actuating rod are visible. The wheel retracted aft into a well that remained covered by two large doors even when the gear was extended. These doors opened only during the extension and retraction cycles.

LEFT LANDING GEAR

An overall photograph of the left main landing gear was taken during a maintenance period on the aircraft. This view clearly illustrates that only one small door remained open when the gear was fully extended. Again, open bomb bay doors can be seen in the background.
(IPMS Spruce Goose Chapter)

Details on the inside of the left main gear wheel are revealed in this close-up. (IPMS Spruce Goose Chapter)

The angles between the strut, link, rod, and door are visible in this rear view. (IPMS Spruce Goose Chapter)

The connecting rod between the strut door and drag link is clearly illustrated here. Protective aluminum colored paint has been applied to all of the components of the gear except for the oleo portion of the main strut.

B-25D COCKPIT DETAILS & COLORS

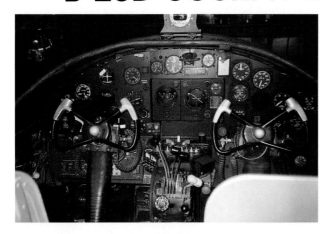

The instrument panel in the B-25D on display at the United States Air Force Museum in Dayton, Ohio, remains much as it was when the aircraft was in service. It was one of the B-25Ds completed as an F-10 photographic reconnaissance aircraft, but it is now displayed with its exterior painted to represent a B-25B used in the Doolittle raid. The fairings for the cameras in the nose have been removed, and some other details have been changed to more closely represent a B-25B. Features of the instrument panel are generally accurate for a B-25D and F-10.

A close-up shows the details of the throttle stand between the pilot's and co-pilot's seats.

Details along the pilot's side of the cockpit included the large radio compass control box. The smaller silver panel is a filter switch, and the larger silver panel is a jack box.

The co-pilot's side also had a jack box and a filter switch. Radio gear was often installed further aft on this side of the cockpit.

The navigator's compartment was immediately aft of the cockpit. This view looks aft into the right side of the compartment.

Details on the left side of the navigator's compartment are visible here. This photograph, and the one to the left, were both taken from the cockpit looking aft.

B-25D NOSE COMPARTMENT

The bombardier had to crawl through this passageway, located beneath the cockpit on the left side of the aircraft, to gain access to the nose compartment.

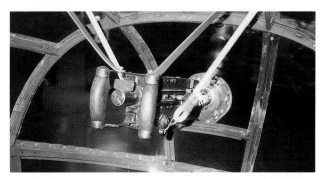

Early versions of the Mitchell had a .30-caliber flexible machine gun mounted in the nose. Elastic cords kept it from moving around on its mount. The two metal braces were added to this museum aircraft to prevent any movement of the gun, but they were not found on operational aircraft.

These panels were on the left side of the nose compartment. The dials include an altimeter and an air speed gage. The bomb release handle is on the floor beneath the electrical panel.

A light switch was located forward on the right side of the nose compartment, and headphones hung just forward of the seat. Ammunition boxes for the .30-caliber machine gun could be stored in the metal brackets.

The small round window was provided to allow the bombardier to reach out and clean the outside of the bomb sight aiming window if it became fogged or dirty. The bomb sight shown here is a replica of the "Woolworth" or aluminum bomb sight developed for the Doolittle raid. It was very simple, yet it was sufficient for that low level mission. Using it also prevented more sophisticated optical sights from falling into the hands of the Japanese.

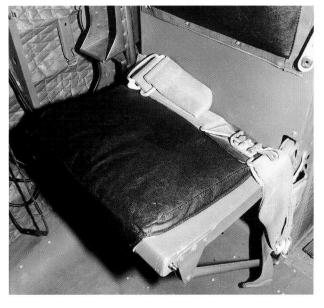

The bombardier rode in this seat in the aft right corner of the compartment. Additional storage brackets for ammunition boxes were located between the seat and the wall.

B-25J NOSE COMPARTMENT

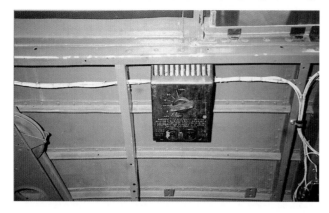

By comparing the details in the nose compartment of a B-25D, as shown on the previous page, with the features in a B-25J, some of the improvements made in the Mitchell's capabilities are apparent. This is a rheostat for Q-18 heated flight suit worn in cold climates. It is on the left side of the nose section, and it was part of the winterization improvements made to later Mitchell variants.

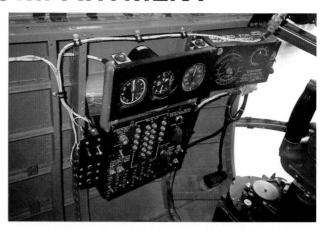

Further forward on the left side were the main control panel, and above it were a compass, altimeter, and air speed indicator. At the center of the panel are bomb indicator lights that tell the bombardier which bombs are present in the bomb bay. The forward-most panel has controls for sequencing the release of the bombs.

Later variants of the Mitchell had a .50-caliber flexible gun in the nose replacing the .30-caliber weapon found in early versions. Because of its heavier weight, it required a mounting frame and a metal plate for its ball socket.

Ammunition for the flexible machine gun was stored in large boxes mounted on a shelf along the right side of the nose compartment. Two fixed .50-caliber machine guns were mounted below the ammunition boxes.

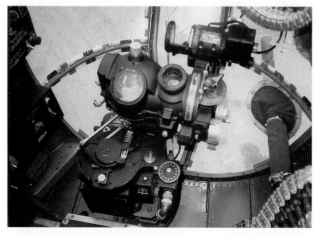

A Norden bomb sight was installed in most versions of the B-25 that were fitted with the standard bombardier's nose compartment, however it was often deleted from Mitchells used primarily or exclusively in the strafer role.
(IPMS Spruce Goose Chapter)

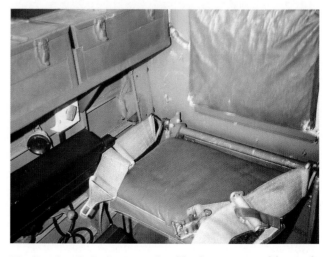

The bombardier's seat remained in the same position as it had previously, and next to it were boxes of .50-caliber machine gun ammunition. The aft ends of the two fixed guns are also visible.

B-25J BOMB BAY DETAILS & COLORS

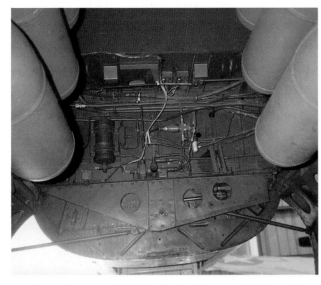

The bomb bay remained basically the same in all versions of the Mitchell. Details at the forward end of the bay in a B-25J are shown here. Note the arms that open and close the doors.

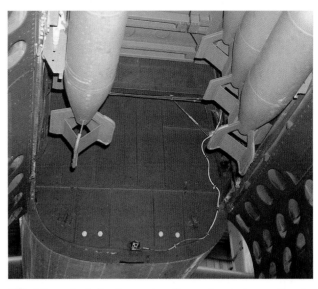

The aft end of the bay was almost featureless. Bombs were usually attached to racks on each side of the bay, but the arrangement of the racks could be varied depending on the number and size of the bombs to be loaded.

Bombs were loaded vertically on structures that looked like ladders on each side of the bomb bay.

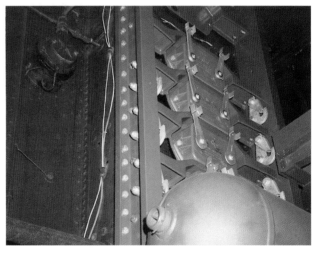

The bombs were attached to natural metal bomb racks fitted on the mounting structures. These racks varried in type according to the size of the bomb that was used. Three empty racks are shown here on the right side of the bomb bay.

The inside of the bomb bay doors were perforated with numerous lightening holes.

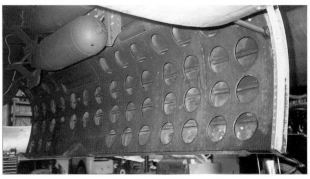

The left bomb bay door was simply a mirror image of the right door.

R-2600 ENGINE DETAILS & COLORS

All variants of the B-25 were powered by the Wright R-2600, fourteen-cylinder, twin-row raidal engine. It provided 1,700 horsepower for take-off, and 1,300 continuous horsepower was developed for cruise at 13,000 feet.

This picture, and the remaining photographs on this page and the next, show the details and colors of the R-2600-29 as used in late B-25Hs and B-25Js. This is the left engine as viewed from the front.

Details and colors inside the engine accessory compartment are shown here. This is the inboard side of the left engine.

Five exhaust stubs on the inside of the left engine are visible in this view. These fit into the small fairings on the cowling's covers.

The accessory compartment for the right engine is shown here from the outboard side with the access panels removed.

Carburetion air was taken into the powerplant through the scoop on top of the nacelle. This is the right engine as viewed from the outboard side.

The inboard side of the right engine was simply a mirror image of that on the left engine.

This view looks into the accessory compartment for the right engine from the inboard side.

BENDIX TOP TURRET DETAILS & COLORS

This Bendix A-9 gun turret, as used in the B-25H and B-25J, is on display at the outstanding Museum of Aviation at Warner Robins, Georgia. This rear view of the turret shows the gunners "bicycle" seat and the posts on which his feet rested as the turret operated. Elevation and azimuth were controlled by the two black grips visible in the turret just above the seat.

A front view of the turret shows the holes in the foot rest supports that allowed the rests to be adjusted to a height that was comfortable for the gunner. The turret was operated by a one-half horsepower electric motor.

When the gunner was seated, his head was actually inside the clear dome, and he viewed his targets through an N-6A gun sight which was mounted between the weapons. At least three different designs of clear domes were used on the B-25H and B-25J as illustrated on page 68. The green color seen on the turret is Dull Dark Green, one of several interior colors used in Mitchells.

Ammunition was contained in the two metal boxes, and 400 rounds were provided for each gun which fired at a rate of 550 rounds per minute. Removable canvas bags were usually attached to the sides of the guns and hung down almost the entire length of the pedestal. They were used to catch the spent shell casings and links as the guns were fired, but they are not present on this turret.

B-25G

The last B-25C-1-NA, 41-13296, was used as the XB-25G developmental aircraft. It was fitted with a shorter solid nose that contained a 75-mm cannon and two .50-caliber machine guns. (National Archives)

Field modifications that added fixed machine guns in the nose compartments of B-25Cs and B-25Ds had proved successful in enhancing the Mitchell's capabilities in the strafer role that was so important in the Pacific theater. The development of the B-25G was a larger and more official effort to take this potential a step further by producing a variant that was designed more specifically for this low level mission. As originally conceived, the B-25G was primarily intended for low-level attacks against shipping.

B-25C-1-NA, 41-13296, became the XB-25G prototype when its standard nose section was replaced with a shorter solid nose. An M4 75-mm cannon, which was nine feet, six inches long, and weighing approximately 900 pounds, was mounted in the former bombardier's crawlway. A special cradle was developed for the cannon, and it had a hydro-spring mechanism to absorb the shock of the twenty-one inch recoil. Some publications have stated that the recoil from firing the weapon was so great that the B-25G almost stopped momentarily in the air as the gun was fired. However, official reports state that the recoil was negligible due to the hydro-spring mechanism. This may well be one of those cases where perception and reality were two different things.

The M4 cannon fired a round which was twenty-six inches long and weighed twenty pounds. Of this, the projectile portion of the round weighed fifteen pounds. Rounds had to be loaded by hand and fired one at a time, but it was believed that the weapon would be very effective, particularly against shipping. The standard load carried was twenty-one rounds, and the task of loading the weapon in combat was assigned to the navigator.

Four-hundred rounds were provided for each of the two .50-caliber machine guns which were also installed

Above: This B-25G was assigned to the 823rd Bomb Squadron of the 38th Bomb Group. A yellow, red, and black tiger's head is painted on the nose. The cowl ring is medium blue, as is the bottom of the vertical tail below the serial number. (USAFM)

Right: Standard armament in the nose of a B-25G included two .50-caliber machine guns and one 75-mm cannon which was mounted in the former bombardier's crawlway. The cannon had to be loaded by hand, one round at a time. (USAFM)

49

An excellent flying view of B-25G-10-NA, 42-65128, reveals standard details for this version of the Mitchell. They include the astrodome above the navigator's station, but no waist or tail gun positions. The two teardrop shaped navigation lights, fitted to early Mitchells on the top and bottom of each wing tip, were replaced by a single light on the very tip of each wing. (USAFM)

in the new nose. During a strafing run, the pilot would use the fire from the two machine guns to line up the target, then he would fire rounds from the cannon as fast as the navigator/cannoneer could load them. The two .50-caliber machine guns also served to suppress enemy fire during the run.

In January 1943, the XB-25G was flown to Columbia, South Carolina, where it began tests against targets in the water off Myrtle Beach. The muzzle blast caused damage to the nose section, so the barrel was lengthened approximately three inches on production aircraft.

Following the XB-25G, five B-25G-1-NA service test aircraft were built by modifying B-25C-15-NA airframes. These were serial numbers 42-32384 through 42-32388. The four hundred production B-25Gs that were then produced were originally ordered as B-25C-20-NAs, but the contract was modified changing these aircraft to B-25Gs. It should be noted that sixty-three existing B-25C airframes were also converted to B-25G standards.

Beginning with B-25G-5-NA, 42-65001, the troublesome and ineffective lower turret was deleted from the production lines, but this left the B-25G with only the top turret as defensive armament. As a result, some B-25Gs had tail gun positions added at modification centers. These looked much like the installation that would become standard on the later B-25H and B-25J, but it was not as deep and had only a single .50-caliber weapon. Waist gun positions, also similar to what would follow on the B-25H and B-25J, were added to some B-25Gs. Photographs provide evidence that some aircraft were fitted with the tail gun positions but not the waist guns.

A minor but noticeable exterior change involved the navigation lights on the wing tips. Earlier versions had a small teardrop shaped light on the top and bottom of each tip panel. During B-25G production, these were replaced by a single larger light mounted on the outer edge of each wing tip.

Another small physical change was the addition of a piece of metal plating in the lower corner of the wind-

B-25C-25-NA, 42-64758, was one of sixty-three Mitchell's originally completed as B-25Cs then converted to B-25G standards. It was painted in the Olive Drab and white sea search camouflage scheme. Dark blue has been painted around the national insignias to cover the previous red surround.
(National Archives)

B-25G-5-NA, 42-64968, was one of several B-25Gs to have waist and tail gun positions added at modification centers. The waist gun positions are very much like those that were standard on the later B-25H and B-25J, although they are open with no perspex in them. At first glance, the tail gun position may look like that used in the later variants, but it is not as wide and has only a single .50-caliber machine gun. (USAFM)

screen on the pilot's side. Its purpose was to serve as a shield to protect the pilot from the flash of the 75-mm cannon. A vertical strip of metal framework was added next to it on the inboard side, and it ran up to the first lateral frame above.

Although B-25Gs were used against ships, they were often employed against ground targets. The slow firing 75-mm cannon was not considered effective for many of these targets. In some cases, it was therefore removed and replaced by two additional .50-caliber machine guns in the field.

Only one B-25G, 42-65031, was acquired by the Navy and redesignated PBJ-1G, BuNo. 35097. A few B-25Gs were transferred to Australia, but otherwise there is no record of any B-25Gs being supplied to the air forces of any other foreign nation. Within the USAAF, training versions of the B-25G were originally designated AT-24Bs, but this was subsequently changed to TB-25G on June 11, 1948.

DATA

Version	B-25G
North American Model Number	NA-96
U. S. Navy/Marine Designation	PBJ-1G*
British Designation	None
Number Built	400**
First Flight	October 22, 1942
First Delivery	May 1943
Last Delivery	August 1943
Powerplants	Wright R-2600-13
Maximum Horsepower (each)	1,700
Maximum Speed	281 mph @ 15,000 feet
Initial Rate of Climb	967 feet per minute
Ceiling	24,300 feet
Combat Range	1,525 miles
Empty Weight	19,975 pounds
Maximum Take-off Weight	35,000 pounds

* Only one PBJ-1G, BuNo. 35097, (ex USAAF Serial number 42-65031) was acquired by the USN Bureau of Aeronautics.
** Additionally, there was one XB-25G prototype and five service test aircraft. Sixty-three existing B-25Cs were also modified to B-25G standards.

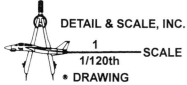

DETAIL & SCALE, INC.

SCALE
1
1/120th
® DRAWING

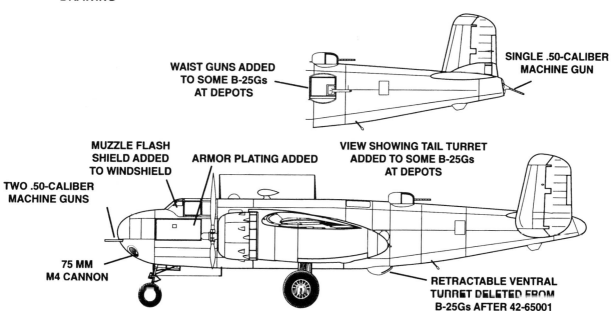

WAIST GUNS ADDED TO SOME B-25Gs AT DEPOTS

SINGLE .50-CALIBER MACHINE GUN

MUZZLE FLASH SHIELD ADDED TO WINDSHIELD

ARMOR PLATING ADDED

VIEW SHOWING TAIL TURRET ADDED TO SOME B-25Gs AT DEPOTS

TWO .50-CALIBER MACHINE GUNS

75 MM M4 CANNON

RETRACTABLE VENTRAL TURRET DELETED FROM B-25Gs AFTER 42-65001

DETAIL & SCALE COPYRIGHT DRAWING BY LLOYD S. JONES

B-25H

The B-25H was an improved version of the B-25G with four .50-caliber machine guns in the nose. The B-25H was also the first Mitchell variant to have enclosed staggered waist gun positions and a twin tail gun position as production standards. The top turret was moved forward so that it was located in the navigator's compartment just aft of the cockpit. This aircraft is B-25H-1-NA, 43-4134. All of the B-25H-1-NAs were delivered with the gun packs only on the right side. (Jones collection)

Operational experience with the B-25G proved that the concept of having a piece of flying artillery was valid. The 75-mm cannon was effective against many types of targets, particularly coastal shipping and even warships up to the size of a destroyer. But the limitations of the B-25G were also quite evident, and to correct these, the B-25H was developed.

Perhaps the most important of the B-25G's shortcomings was the lack of defensive armament, particularly after the lower turret was deleted during production. Although the addition of tail and waist gun positions at depots helped some, they were not the real answer. Part of the problem was that the top turret was located in the aft fuselage compartment, so it prevented effective movement of any waist guns which were also added in that cramped space.

To solve this problem in the B-25H, the top turret was moved forward to the navigator's compartment just aft of the cockpit. This meant that the ADF "football" antenna had to be moved to a location under the forward fuselage, and the astrodome and side scanning windows in the navigator's compartment were eliminated. Two small fairings were added on top of the fuselage just aft of the gun muzzles when the turret was in the stowed position pointing aft. These fairings were actually pieces of armor that deflected bullets away from the tail gunner's position in the event the guns in the top turret were accidently fired while in this stowed position.

Moving the turret forward left the rear fuselage compartment open for more effective use of waist guns. Staggered waist gun positions were added which were slightly bulged and covered with perspex. A .50-caliber machine gun was mounted through an opening in the lower aft corner of each window, and the opening was sealed by a canvas boot around the barrel. The radio operator, who also operated the cameras in the aft fuselage compartment, manned both guns as dictated by the combat situation, and he had good freedom of movement with the top turret no longer in the way. Ammunition was fed to the guns through chutes from overhead storage boxes containing 200 rounds for each weapon. Contrary to what has been stated in at least two other publications, the navigator/cannoneer in the B-25H was not the radio operator, although some radio gear was moved to a box where the co-pilot's rudder pedals were

B-25H-5-NA, 43-4448, has a K-24, 12-inch aim-pointing camera added in the nose just above the four machine guns. Although this camera protrudes forward from the nose of the aircraft, other B-25Hs had cameras that were mounted entirely inside the nose. Two single gun packs have been added to the side of the forward fuselage. (National Archives)

Beginning with the B-25H-5-NA, gun packs were on both sides of the fuselage. Late in the war, these were often removed, because they caused damage to the fuselage structure even when reinforcing plates were added.
(National Archives)

located on other versions. Most of the radio gear and the radio operator himself remained in the aft fuselage compartment.

With B-25H production, a suitable and effective tail turret was finally installed on the Mitchell. To accommodate it, the depth of the aft fuselage was increased by seven inches. The Bell electro-hydraulic turret contained two .50-caliber machine guns with 600 rounds of ammunition provided for each weapon. The gunner sat on a stool under a framed greenhouse that was similar to the one installed at depots to some B-25Cs, Ds, and Gs, however the production tail turret on the B-25H and B-25J was a little wider and deeper than the earlier installation. With the addition of the tail and waist gun positions, the defensive armament of the Mitchell was optimized. Further, during attacks against surface targets, the top turret gunner could train his weapons straight ahead to augment the fire of the guns in the nose.

The number of .50-caliber machine guns mounted inside the nose compartment was increased to four as compared to only two in the B-25G. The 300 B-25H-1-NAs had two single gun packs on the right side of the forward fuselage, but no packs were installed on the left. Subsequent production blocks had two guns on both sides. Therefore, when using the top turret guns to fire forward, a B-25H from the two later production blocks could bring ten .50-caliber machine guns and the 75-mm

cannon to bear on its target. The cannon installed in the B-25H was the T13E1 version which was lighter than the M4 used in the B-25G. However, it still had to be loaded manually and fired one round at a time. As with the B-25G, the cannon was sometimes removed in the field and replaced with two .50-caliber machine guns when those weapons were more suitable for the mission than the larger cannon.

The co-pilot's station was deleted, and the seat was cut down and used by the navigator/cannoneer. The co-pilot's yoke and rudder pedals were removed, and the instrument panel was rearranged for use by a single pilot. Bomb release equipment was located in the cockpit for use by the pilot since there was no bombardier. An A-1 pilot bomb sight was mounted on an N2B gun sight, and it was intended for minimum altitude bombing. As a back-up, a ring and bead sight was also installed just to the right of the N2B. A fold-down chart board was also provided for the navigator/cannoneer for use as he sat in the cut down right seat.

The B-25H was also the first version of the Mitchell to have pilot armor plate added as a production standard. On the exterior of the aircraft, the carburetor air intakes above the engine nacelles were enlarged, and the shrouds on the two right oil cooler vents were deleted. A circular emergency escape hatch was added on the right side of the aft fuselage

"Barbie III" was a B-25H-1-NA assigned to the 1st Air Commando Group in the China, Burma, India Theater. Again, note the lack of gun packs on the left side of these B-25H-1-NAs. *(USAFM)*

The reinforcing plates just forward of the gun packs were used to protect the fuselage from the muzzle blast. At first, these had a layer of felt between them and the fuselage, but the felt hardened after it became wet, thus reducing its effectiveness. Consequently, it was replaced with rubber, but the effects of the gun blast on the fuselage continued to be a problem. (Jones collection)

Electric bomb controls and a gun sight aiming camera were added starting with B-25H-5-NA production. Beginning with B-25H-5-NA, 43-4535, the provision to carry a 2,000-pound bomb was deleted.

B-25C-10-NA, 42-32372, was converted to serve as the XB-25H prototype, and it was followed by 1,000 production aircraft. They were divided into three production blocks of 300 B-25H-1-NAs, 300 B-25H-5-NAs, and 400 B-25H-10-NAs. The last B-25H-10-NA to roll off of the assembly line was also the last Mitchell produced at Inglewood, California. It was named "OLD BONES," and it was signed by the workers who helped build it. It later served with the 81st Bomb Squadron of the 12th Bomb Group still carrying the names on its natural metal skin. The subsequent B-25J variant was produced at Kansas City, Missouri.

The U. S. Navy obtained 236 B-25Hs and redesignated them PBJ-1H. They were used extensively in the anti-shipping role by Marine squadrons in the Pacific. Others flew sea patrol missions along the coast lines of the United States, and one was used for carrier suitability experiments aboard USS SHANGRI-LA, CV-38.

DATA

Version	B-25H
North American Model Number	NA-98
U. S. Navy/Marine Designation	PBJ-1H*
British Designation	None
Number Built	1,000
First Flight	May 15, 1943
First Delivery	August 1943
Last Delivery	July 1944
Powerplant	Wright R-2600-13
Maximum Horsepower (each)	1,700
Maximum Speed	275 mph @ 13,000 feet
Initial Rate of Climb	790 feet per minute
Ceiling	24,800 feet
Ferry Range	2,700 miles
Empty Weight	19,975 pounds
Maximum Take-off Weight	33,500 pounds

* 236 PBJ-1Hs were acquired by the USN Bureau of Aeronautics.

B-25H-5-NA, 43-4460, was stripped of all armament and used by the Air Weather Service once its combat career was finished. (USAFM)

PBJ-1H

The U. S. Navy acquired 236 B-25Hs and redesignated them PBJ-1Hs. As was the case with other versions of the PBJ-1, most were used by the Marines. Some PBJ-1Hs had a search radar mounted on the right wing tip, while other aircraft had a radome on the nose. Still others had no radome at all. *(National Archives)*

To evaluate the possibility of using PBJ-1s aboard carriers, arresting gear and catapult bridle hooks were added to PBJ-1H, BuNo. 35277. Lt. Cdr. H. S. Bottomley made a successful recovery aboard the USS SHANGRI-LA, CV-38. In all, seventeen arrested recoveries and launches were made over a two day period. *(National Archives)*

After being freed from the arresting cable, Lt. Cdr. Bottomley taxied forward on the SHANGRI-LA's flight deck toward the catapults. Appropriately, the SHANGRI-LA was named for the mythical base President Franklin D. Roosevelt once claimed Doolittle's B-25Bs had used for their famous raid. *(National Archives)*

The PBJ-1H was then hooked up to catapult number 1. Other than the carrier equipment, this PBJ-1H was a standard operational aircraft. *(National Archives)*

The PBJ-1H was then successfully launched from SHAN-GRI-LA, but the Navy did not continue the development of PBJ-1s for carrier operations. *(National Archives)*

NOSE ARMAMENT

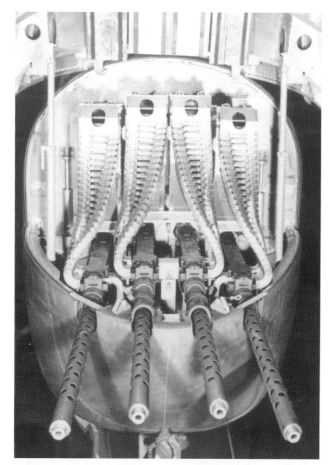

Above left and right: Details of the machine gun compartment in the nose of a B-25H are visible in these two views. In the photo at right, the ammunition boxes and the feed chutes have been removed. Note that the middle two guns are slightly higher than the two outer weapons. *(Both National Archives)*

B-25H-1-NAs only had gun packs on the right side of the forward fuselage, but they were added to left side starting with the first B-25H-5-NA. Note the small round opening for the flush-mounted combat camera just above the four machine guns in the nose. The metal plate in the lower corner of the windshield on the pilot's side is also visible. *(USAFM)*

This B-25H was modified by the Armament Laboratory of the Air Technical Service Command at Wright Field, Ohio. The 75-mm cannon was replaced with two weapons called rocket guns, and a single rocket gun was also fitted under the forward fuselage. These rocket guns should not be confused with the standard 4.5-inch triple rocket tubes used on several U. S. aircraft and also evaluated for use on the B-25H. The rocket gun test did not lead to their operational use. *(National Archives)*

COCKPIT DETAILS

The B-25H had a pilot but no co-pilot. The co-pilot's control yoke and rudder pedals were replaced with a box containing radio equipment. The loader for the 75-mm cannon sat in a cut down seat and placed his feet on a slanted board just aft of the box.

(National Archives)

Details on the left side of the cockpit of a B-25H are revealed in this view. *(National Archives)*

Part of the cut down loader's seat and the slanted foot board are shown in this photograph of the right side of the cockpit. *(National Archives)*

B-25H, 1/120th SCALE, MULTI-VIEW DRAWINGS

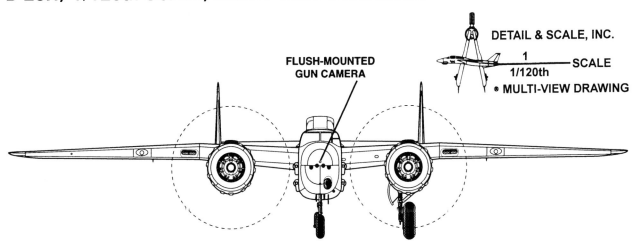

FLUSH-MOUNTED GUN CAMERA

DETAIL & SCALE, INC.

1

1/120th —— SCALE

⊛ MULTI-VIEW DRAWING

DETAIL & SCALE, COPYRIGHT, MULTI-VIEW DRAWINGS BY LLOYD S. JONES

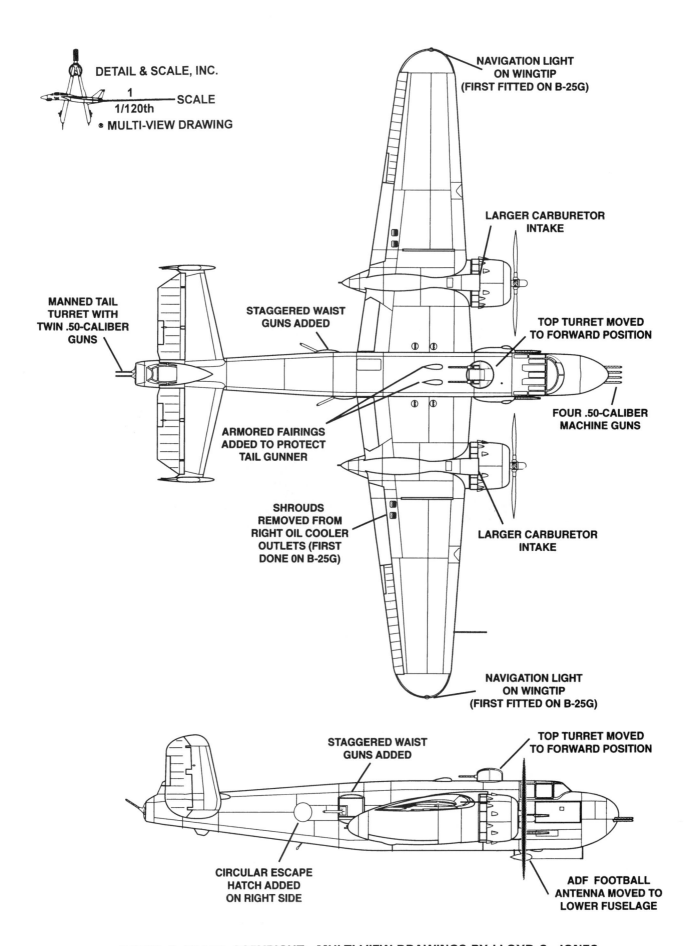

DETAIL & SCALE, INC.

$\frac{1}{1/120th}$ SCALE

● MULTI-VIEW DRAWING

NAVIGATION LIGHT
ON WINGTIP
(FIRST FITTED ON B-25G)

LARGER CARBURETOR
INTAKE

MANNED TAIL
TURRET WITH
TWIN .50-CALIBER
GUNS

STAGGERED WAIST
GUNS ADDED

TOP TURRET MOVED
TO FORWARD POSITION

ARMORED FAIRINGS
ADDED TO PROTECT
TAIL GUNNER

FOUR .50-CALIBER
MACHINE GUNS

SHROUDS
REMOVED FROM
RIGHT OIL COOLER
OUTLETS (FIRST
DONE ON B-25G)

LARGER CARBURETOR
INTAKE

NAVIGATION LIGHT
ON WINGTIP
(FIRST FITTED ON B-25G)

STAGGERED WAIST
GUNS ADDED

TOP TURRET MOVED
TO FORWARD POSITION

CIRCULAR ESCAPE
HATCH ADDED
ON RIGHT SIDE

ADF FOOTBALL
ANTENNA MOVED TO
LOWER FUSELAGE

DETAIL & SCALE, COPYRIGHT, MULTI-VIEW DRAWINGS BY LLOYD S. JONES

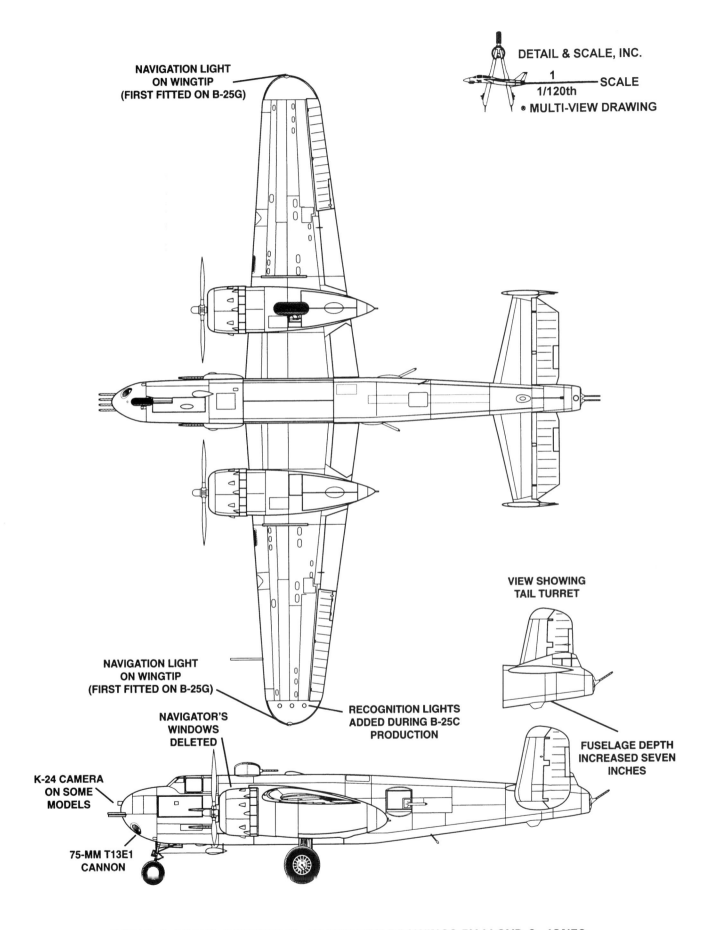

NAVIGATION LIGHT
ON WINGTIP
(FIRST FITTED ON B-25G)

DETAIL & SCALE, INC.

1

SCALE

1/120th

◦ MULTI-VIEW DRAWING

NAVIGATION LIGHT
ON WINGTIP
(FIRST FITTED ON B-25G)

RECOGNITION LIGHTS
ADDED DURING B-25C
PRODUCTION

VIEW SHOWING
TAIL TURRET

NAVIGATOR'S
WINDOWS
DELETED

FUSELAGE DEPTH
INCREASED SEVEN
INCHES

K-24 CAMERA
ON SOME
MODELS

75-MM T13E1
CANNON

DETAIL & SCALE, COPYRIGHT, MULTI-VIEW DRAWINGS BY LLOYD S. JONES

B-25J

The B-25J was the definitive version of the Mitchell, and it was also produced in the greatest numbers. Note the black under-wing bomb racks on this factory fresh aircraft. **(National Archives)**

The final production version of the Mitchell was the B-25J, and it was ordered in larger numbers than any other variant. A total of 4,318 were delivered, and most of these had the framed glass bombardier's nose that had been standard on all versions prior to the B-25G. An additional seventy-two aircraft were completed as the war came to the end, but they were not delivered contractually. Later, some of these were modified for other missions and served in the post war years.

For use in the strafer role, some B-25Js were completed with solid noses that contained eight .50-caliber machine guns in two vertical rows of four. Solid nose kits were also produced separately and delivered for conversion to this gun nose configuration in the field. Defensive armament remained the same as it had been on the B-25H, and this included the top turret located forward in the navigator's compartment, the two staggered waist gun positions, and the twin tail turret.

The A-1 bombing head remained on the N3B or N3C gun sight and was retained for use in low level bombing attacks. The cockpit was returned to the dual configuration with seats and controls set up for both a pilot and co-pilot. Instruments were rearranged and optimized for two-pilot operations. The flash shield in the lower corner of the pilot's windshield, that had first been installed on the B-25G and continued on the B-25H, remained on most B-25Js, although this version did not carry the 75-mm cannon. On some aircraft, the metal plate was removed and replaced with a clear section of perspex which had a metal frame running horizontally across the top.

The bomb bay was revised so that the number of 1,000-pound bombs that could be carried was increased from two to three. Two 1,600-pound armor piercing bombs could also be loaded for use against hardened targets. The capability for carrying six 325-pound depth charges on racks under the wings was also added. Beginning with B-25J-1-NC, 43-4019, the provision for

carrying a 2,000-pound bomb was deleted.

Most references state that the B-25J had the strap-on gun pack on the forward fuselage, but this is an oversimplification of the facts and is not really accurate. The 555 B-25J-1-NCs were delivered without the side gun packs on either side of the fuselage. These were restored on later production blocks, but they were often removed in the field, because the stress to the fuselage caused by the muzzle blast continued to be a problem.

Beginning with B-25J-5-NC, 43-27793, the N3B gun sight was replaced with the N3C, but the A-1 bombing head was retained. Later, the N3C would be replaced with the N9B during B-25J-30-NC production. Deicing windshield panels were fitted as were blast arresters on the top turret's guns. Starting with B-25J-10-NC, 43-35995, electrically operated bomb racks and doors were installed, and from B-25J-15-NC, 44-28711, optical sights were added to the waist guns.

On B-25J-20-NC, 44-29111, and subsequent B-25Js, a second fixed .50-caliber machine gun was added on the right inside the bombardier's nose compartment as a production standard. This second gun had also been installed on many existing aircraft at the field depot at Townsville, Australia. On some aircraft, a second pair of fixed machine guns was installed in the left side of the nose in an arrangement that mirrored the guns on the right. This modification was also carried out at Towns-

These B-25Js were photographed at Mar Strip, Cape Sansapor in Dutch New Guinea during September 1944. **(National Archives)**

Although most B-25Js had the standard bombardier's nose, some were completed with solid noses containing eight .50-caliber machine guns. North American also produced kits so these noses could be fitted to existing B-25Js in the field. These aircraft were assigned to the 405th Bomb Squadron of the 38th Bomb Group. A color side profile of the aircraft in the background appears on page 34. (USAFM)

ville. These four guns, along with the flexible gun in the center of the nose, generated considerable gas inside the nose when fired. As a result, a gun gas extractor had to be installed in a fairing under the nose to remove it. This extractor was also added to some B-25Js having only the two right side guns and the flexible gun in the nose.

Also during production of the B-25J-20-NC, the dome for the top turret was reinforced with metal framework at the back, the mount for the flexible gun in the nose was raised four inches, and armor protection was added for the bombardier. New armored seats were provided for the pilot and co-pilot beginning with B-25J-25-NC, 44-29911. The plates of armor were hinged to allow easier access into the cockpit.

Improvements in armament capabilities continued to be made as production proceeded, and these included provisions for T-64 zero-length launchers under the wings to carry 5-inch rockets beginning with B-25J-30-NC, 44-31338. Shortly thereafter, on 44-31491, a K-10 lead-computing sight and an M8A gun mount were installed in the tail turret. Provisions for glide bombing were added starting with 44-86692. Finally, beginning with B-25J-35-NC, 44-86892, the capability to carry and deploy aerial mines was added.

The U. S. Navy's Bureau of Aeronautics took delivery of 244 B-25Js which it redesignated PBJ-1Js. This was the largest number of any Mitchell variant acquired by the Navy. Many had search radars added to their starboard wing tips or to the top of their nose, and a few aircraft assigned to VMB-612 were modified to carry two Tiny Tim rockets on the sides of the fuselage next to the bomb bay.

The Royal Air Force acquired 314 B-25Js which it named the Mitchell III. Other nations using the B-25J during the war included Australia, Brazil, China, Canada, and The Netherlands. After the war Argentina received

A close-up shows how the eight .50-caliber machine guns were mounted vertically in the nose. (USAFM)

Above: These PBJ-1Js are painted in the tri-color camouflage scheme and have radomes on their starboard wing tips. They also have the bombardier's nose which was standard on most PBJ-1Js. (USAFM)

Right: PBJ-1Js assigned to VMB-612 on Iwo Jima were also fitted with the standard bombardier's nose, but the glass has been painted over, and a radome has been installed at the top of the nose section. The aircraft is painted in the overall Glossy Sea Blue scheme. VMB-612's aircraft were modified to carry the Tiny Tim rocket on mounts outside the bomb bay, and two of these rockets can be seen on this aircraft. (National Archives)

three B-25Js for private use, while the air forces of Chile, Columbia, Mexico, Peru, Uruguay, and Venezuela all operated relatively small numbers of B-25Js.

The first use of Mitchells in non-combat roles began during World War II when several VIP transports were converted from standard airframes. Originally called RB-25s (the "R" standing for restricted), two of these went to Generals Henry "Hap" Arnold and Dwight D. "Ike" Eisenhower. More transports were converted after the war when the designation was changed to VB-25. The RB-25 designation was then applied to remaining F-10 reconnaissance aircraft so that the "F" designator could be used for fighter aircraft. Both VB-25J and VB-25N VIP transports were converted.

The B-25's airframe proved quite adaptable for other uses after the war, and many became trainers. Wartime training versions of the B-25J had been designated AT-24D, but in June 1948, this was changed to TB-25J. Some of these were used for multi-engine transition or refresher training, and the TB-25L designation was often applied. Others had radar systems installed to train operators, and these included the TB-25K trainer for the Hughes E-1 radar/fire control system and the TB-25M for the E-5 system. JB-25Js, JTB-25Js, and JTB-25Ns were used for a variety of special tests. Other Mitchells served in the post-war years as hack or utility aircraft towing

targets and performing other day-to-day non-combat roles.

DATA

Version	B-25J
North American Model Number	NA-108
U. S. Navy/Marine Designation	PBJ-1J*
British Designations	Mitchell III
Number Delivered	4,318**
First Flight	December 14, 1943
First Delivery	December 1943
Last Delivery	August 1945
Powerplant	Wright R-2600-29
Maximum Horsepower (each)	1,700
Maximum Speed	293 mph @ 13,850 feet
Initial Rate of Climb	1,587 feet per minute
Ceiling	24,500 feet
Ferry Range	3,240 miles
Empty Weight	19,490 pounds
Maximum Take-off Weight	33,400 pounds

* 244 PBJ-1Js were acquired by the USN Bureau of Aeronautics.
** 4,390 built, but only 4,318 delivered.

Left: Whether fitted with the standard bombardier's nose or the solid gun nose, the B-25J had a cockpit with both pilot and co-pilot. The layout of the instruments remained basically the same as it had been in versions prior to the B-25H. (USAFM)

Below left and right: Details on the cockpit side walls are illustrated in these two views. Some of the equipment is the same as it had been since the first B-25s were built, but other items varied even between the production blocks of B-25Js.
(National Archives)

B-25J, 1/120th SCALE, MULTI-VIEW DRAWINGS

DETAIL & SCALE, INC.

$\frac{1}{\text{1/120th}}$ SCALE

● MULTI-VIEW DRAWING

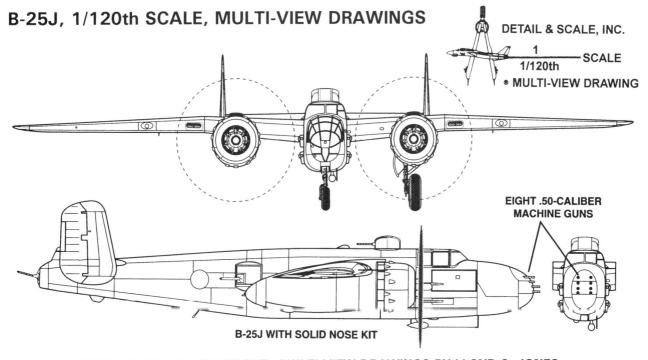

EIGHT .50-CALIBER MACHINE GUNS

B-25J WITH SOLID NOSE KIT

DETAIL & SCALE, COPYRIGHT, MULTI-VIEW DRAWINGS BY LLOYD S. JONES

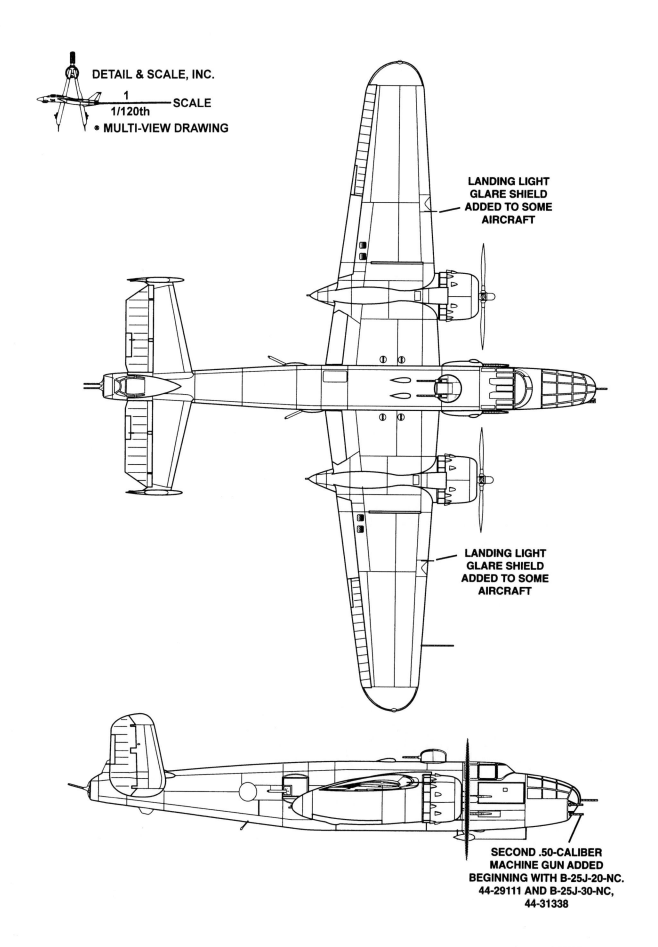

DETAIL & SCALE, INC.

1
———— SCALE
1/120th

• MULTI-VIEW DRAWING

LANDING LIGHT
GLARE SHIELD
ADDED TO SOME
AIRCRAFT

LANDING LIGHT
GLARE SHIELD
ADDED TO SOME
AIRCRAFT

SECOND .50-CALIBER
MACHINE GUN ADDED
BEGINNING WITH B-25J-20-NC.
44-29111 AND B-25J-30-NC,
44-31338

DETAIL & SCALE, COPYRIGHT, MULTI-VIEW DRAWINGS BY LLOYD S. JONES

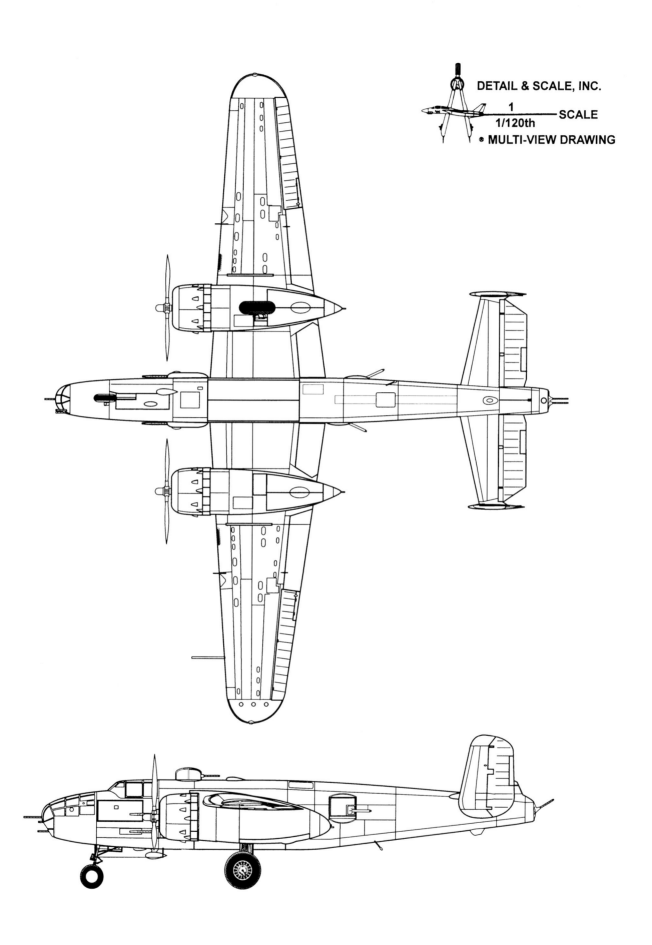

DETAIL & SCALE, INC.

1
──────── SCALE
1/120th

* MULTI-VIEW DRAWING

POST WAR VARIANTS

This B-25J has the Strategic Air Command's "Milky Way" band on its nose, but it served as a utility aircraft rather than a bomber. *(USAFM)*

Numerous B-25Js were modified after the war for special purposes, and often the designations were changed. The aircraft illustrated on this page are representative examples of post-war Mitchells. This B-25J retained its original designation and served as a hack aircraft with the 4708th Air Defense Wing at Selfridge AFB, Michigan, in the mid-1950s. *(USAFM)*

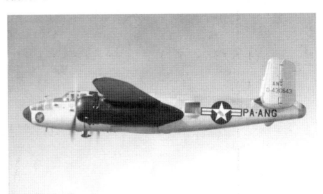

B-25Js used as trainers for the Hughes E-1 Radar/Fire Control System were redesignated TB-25Ks. This one was operated by the Michigan Air National Guard. *(USAFM)*

This TB-25K was used as a training aircraft by the Pennsylvania ANG. Note the solid black radome on the nose of this aircraft and the one in the photograph to the left. *(USAFM)*

TB-25Ms were B-25Js converted for use as trainers for the Hughes E-5 Radar/Fire Control System. Markings for the Wisconsin ANG are on the nose. *(USAFM)*

Former B-25Js used for multi-engine pilot training were redesignated TB-25Ns. This one was flown by the Missouri Air Guard. *(USAFM)*

This TB-25N was retained for use as a trainer by the active Air Force. *(USAFM)*

SAC used this VB-25N as a VIP transport. It was one of twenty-seven VB-25N conversions. *(USAFM)*

MITCHELL DETAILS

ARMAMENT DETAILS

NOSE GUNS & STRAP ON PODS

The original .30-caliber flexible machine gun in the bombardier's compartment was replaced with a .50-caliber weapon beginning with the B-25C-5-NA and the B-25D-5-NC. At the same time, a fixed .50-caliber machine gun was also added on the right side of the nose compartment.

The fixed machine guns in the nose were fed with ammunition stored in boxes on the floor under the bombardier's seat.

Gun packs were often added to the sides of the forward fuselage. This dual gun pack was the first to be used, and it was often seen on early PBJ-1s, B-25Cs, and B-25Ds. As the guns were fired, links were ejected through the two smaller holes, while spent shell casings were expended through the larger holes. Both single and dual gun packs were originally made at Townsville, Australia, but they were later produced by Consolidated.

A second fixed .50-caliber machine gun was added on the right side of the bombardier's compartment beginning with B-25J-20-NC, 44-29111. This was a production standard, but in the field, two additional guns were sometimes installed on the left side in an arrangement that mirrored that on the right.

The more common side gun packs were single units mounted in pairs on each side. Some B-25Hs and B-25Js were produced with these packs only on the right side, but most had them on both sides of the forward fuselage. Note the reinforcing plates intended to protect the fuselage structure from the muzzle blast. The cover has been removed from the lower gun pack in this photo.

(National Archives)

TOP TURRET

There were several different designs for the clear dome on the top turret used on the B-25H and B-25J. This dome is almost completely clear and lacks any metal framework. The slots for the barrels were covered from the inside by curved pieces of metal as seen on the mount in the photograph below. The two fairings aft of the gun barrels were pieces of armor added to the top of the fuselage to deflect bullets away from the tail gun position if the turret guns were fired to the rear by accident.

(National Archives)

The rear of this dome has been re-enforced with metal framework that is painted the same color as the aircraft's fuselage, but the shape of the dome itself remains basically symmetrical like the one shown above.

(National Archives)

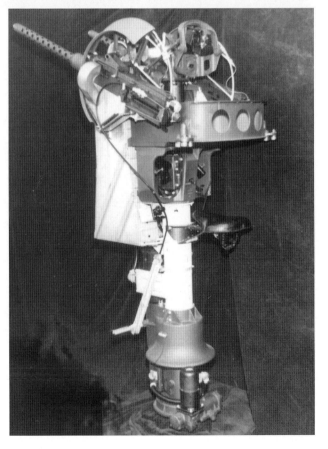

Above: The dome on this turret is more asymmetrical in shape that the two shown above, and the gun barrels are mounted in slots covered by clear perspex rather than the usual curved pieces of metal. The gun sight is clearly visible beneath the dome.   (USAFM)

Right: This view of the turret shows the curved pieces of metal that filled in the slots for the barrels in the domes illustrated in the two top photographs above. Color pictures of the turret can be found on page 48.

(National Archives)

WAIST GUNS

The B-25H and B-25J had staggered waist gun windows that were slightly bulged and covered with clear perspex. The gun was mounted through an opening at the lower aft corner of the window, and a canvas boot sealed the opening around the gun barrel. This is the right waist gun position, and it was further forward than the one on the left.

This view looks forward into the radio operator's compartment, and the feed chutes for both waist guns are visible. Ammunition was fed from boxes mounted high on the sides of the fuselage. Spent links and shell casings were ejected from the gun into canvas bags which were olive drab in color. *(National Archives)*

This photograph was taken from the radio operator's compartment, and it looks aft. The two .50-caliber waist guns were mounted on gray frames which were attached to the fuselage structure. The boxes on the side of the fuselage in the background contained ammunition for the tail gun turret. *(National Archives)*

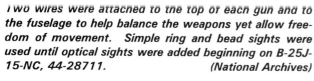

Two wires were attached to the top of each gun and to the fuselage to help balance the weapons yet allow freedom of movement. Simple ring and bead sights were used until optical sights were added beginning on B-25J-15-NC, 44-28711. *(National Archives)*

Details of the left waist gun are illustrated in this view. Extra ammunition boxes could be stored along the sides of the aircraft further aft. Both this photograph, and the one to the left, were taken from the radio operator's compartment looking aft. *(National Archives)*

TAIL GUN POSITION

Above left: The tail gun position as used in the B-25H and B-25J is shown here with the top hatch on the gunner's greenhouse removed. Note the canvas boot around the gun barrels. (National Archives)

Above right: In this photograph, the hatch is in place, but the aft cover and canvas boot have been removed to show the guns and the chutes that fed ammunition to them. (National Archives)

Left: The armor plate that protected the tail gunner is shown in this view that looks down into the tail gun position. The gun sight is visible at the top of the photo, while the two pistol grips that controlled the tail gun turret can be seen at the bottom. (National Archives)

The tail gunner sat on a short stool with a canvas covered pad. Seat belts for the gunner are on the floor just forward of the stool. (IPMS Spruce Goose Chapter)

The streamlined shape of the housing above the tail gun position is evident in this external view which looks aft. (IPMS Spruce Goose Chapter

WING DETAILS

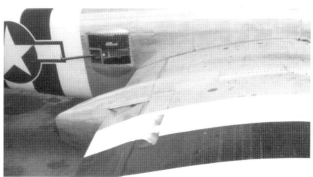

Details on top of the left wing are visible here. The two vents for the left oil cooler can be seen in the nearest white stripe and part of the first black stripe. The small fence on the leading edge of the wing was only on a few B-25Js, and it was to help prevent the landing/taxi light from shining into the bombardier's compartment.
(IPMS Spruce Goose Chapter)

On early versions of the Mitchell, the two vents for the oil cooler on the top of the right wing were covered by shrouds. These were deleted on the B-25G, B-25H, and B-25J, leaving the two vents with the same appearance as those on the left wing. Small round fuel filler caps were located inboard and outboard of the engine nacelle.
(IPMS Spruce Goose Chapter)

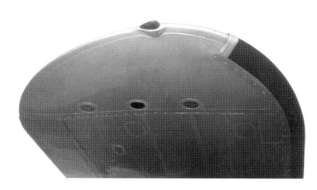

Early Mitchells had navigation lights on the top and bottom of each wing tip panel. Beginning with the B-25G, these were replaced with a single light right on the edge of each wing tip as shown here. The three identification lights first appeared under the right wing tip on the B-25C and B-25D, and they remained a standard feature for all subsequent variants.

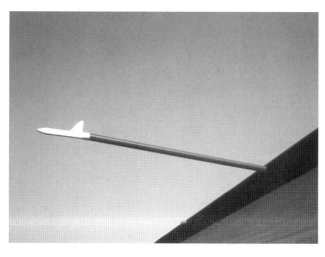

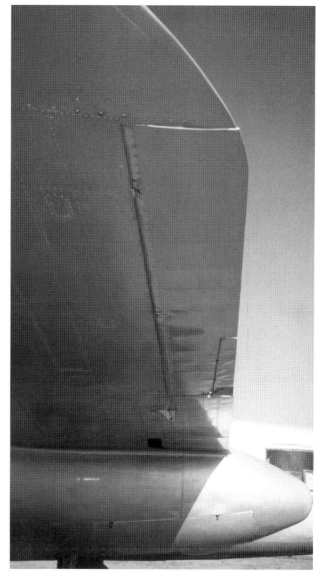

The pitot probe was located on the leading edge of the right wing on all versions of the Mitchell.

Both of the large fabric covered ailerons had moveable trim tabs at their inboard end next to the outer flaps.

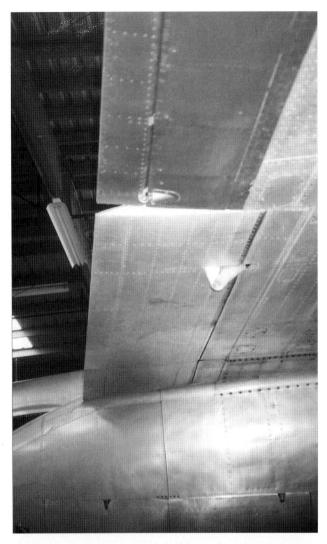

The outer right flap is shown here in the lowered position.

This is the outer left flap in the lowered position.

Each wing had two flaps, which were on both sides of the engine nacelle. This is the outer flap on the right wing in the raised position. Note the single hinge near the outer end of the flap.

The two inner flaps were located between the engine nacelles and the fuselage. This is the left inner flap in the lowered position. Note the angle on the outboard end of the trailing edge.

This is the right inner flap. This photograph, and the one to the left, provide a look at the scanning windows for the radio operator's position as found on the B-25D and F-10.

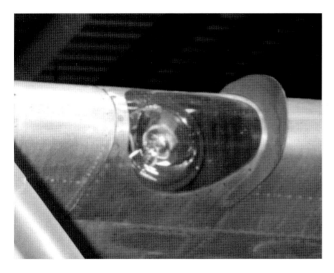

All versions of the Mitchell had landing/taxi lights on the leading edge of each outer wing panel. On some B-25Js, a shield to reduce glare into the bombardier's compartment was added as shown here. This is the light on the right wing.

The oil coolers were buried in the wings outboard of the engine nacelles. The air scoop for the oil cooler in the right wing is shown here. Deicing boots were often removed from aircraft in the field.

Above left: The access panel for the left oil cooler has been removed, and the core style radiator is visible aft of the scoop for the cooling air. The ducting to the radiator has also been removed.

Above right: This is the left oil cooler, and again the access panel has been removed. A protective insert keeps foreign objects out of the scoop on the leading edge of the wing.

Right: This close-up shows how the ducting running back from the air scoop was attached to the front of the radiator core of the oil cooler.

FUSELAGE DETAILS

The forward window on each side of the cockpit slid aft to provide cooling air while on the ground in hot climates. It also allowed the pilots to talk to ground crew personnel.

Small scoops on the sides of the forward fuselage provided cooling air for the forward compartments when the aircraft was in flight. The location and number of these scoops varied on different versions of the Mitchell.

A forward-looking camera could be mounted inside the cockpit on the right side of the windscreen. It could be used for documentation or training purposes.
(National Archives)

On the B-25H and B-25J, a circular escape hatch was located on the right side of the fuselage just aft of the waist gun. It is shown here with the panel removed.
(National Archives)

Some B-25s had a windshield wiper on the aiming window for the bomb sight. The small circular window, which could be opened in flight to allow the bombardier to reach out and wipe off the aiming window, remained a standard feature on all versions of the Mitchells with the bombardier's nose. It was located just to the right of the top of the bomb aiming window.

On the B-25H and B-25J, a small bulge was added to the larger nose landing gear door. Although the specified size of the nose wheel tire did not increase, the change to a more aggressive tread design required the extra clearance.

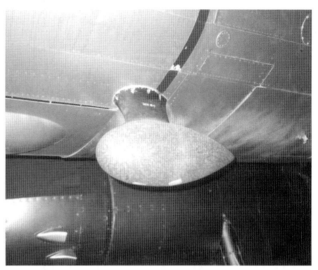

Because the top turret was moved forward to the navigator's compartment on the B-25H and B-25J, the ADF "football" antenna had to be moved to a position under the forward fuselage.

Entry to the Mitchell's forward and aft compartments was provided by two rectangular hatches under the fuselage that hinged at their forward end. Steps were built into the hatches to allow the crew members to climb up into the fuselage. This is the forward entry hatch as seen from the rear.

A small white position light was located under the aft fuselage.

Beginning with the B-25C, a fixed tail bumper fairing became standard on all versions of the Mitchell.

NACELLE DETAILS

Except for the change in the exhaust system and the addition of exhaust stubs around the cowling, the design of the engine nacelles was changed very little throughout the entire production run of B-25s.   (National Archives)

This view shows the open cowl flaps and the exhaust stubs on a B-25H.   (National Archives)

The two doors for each main landing gear remained closed under the aft end of each nacelle except when the gear was extending or retracting. Note the bulge at the center of the doors to provide clearance for the tire.

A close-up reveals the exhaust stubs under the fairings on the cowling of a B-25D.

Fuel vents were added at the aft end of each nacelle beginning with the B-25C.

TAIL DETAILS

Once the design for the vertical tails was established during flight testing of the first B-25, it remained unchanged for all versions of the Mitchell that followed. Note the small position light just forward of the rudder hinge line inside the horizontal stripes. This light was on the outside of both vertical tails.

Each of the elevators had moveable trim tabs that were controlled by actuators on both the upper and lower surfaces. This is the top of the right elevator.
(National Archives)

Both rudders had trim tabs that had actuators on the inside surface. The hinge slots between the rudder and vertical stabilizer are also visible in this inside view of the left vertical tail.

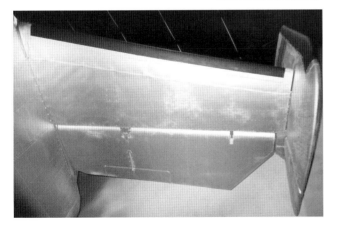

The left horizontal tail is shown here from below. Note the trim tab and its actuator as well as the two hinge slots. The outer edge of each elevator was tapered considerably to allow movement of the rudders.

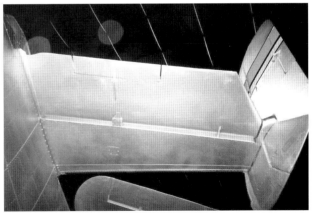

An underside view of the right horizontal tail shows the hinge points as well as the trim tab and its actuator. Like the ailerons, the rudders and elevators on the Mitchell were covered with fabric.

MODELERS SUMMARY

Note: Each volume in Detail & Scale's, "In Detail" series of publications has a Modelers Summary in the back of the book. The Modelers Summary will discuss the injection-molded plastic model kits of the aircraft covered by the book, and all common modeling scales from 1/144th through 1/32nd scale will be included. Highlights of the better kits in each scale will be discussed, and recommendations will be made with respect to which kit or kits in each scale are the best for the serious scale modeler to use. Once a kit has been purchased, the modeler should compare the various features of the kit to the drawings and photographs in the book to determine how accurately specific features are represented. He can then decide what, if any, correcting or detailing work he wants to do to enhance the appearance of the model.

GENERAL

Although quite a few models of the B-25 Mitchell have been released since plastic modeling became popular in the 1950s, very few of them are quality kits that are desirable for use by serious scale modelers. Only one kit is available in 1/144th scale, and just one of the 1/72nd scale kits is very accurate. In 1/48th scale, modelers have a good choice of kits from Accurate Miniatures and Revell-Monogram for building Mitchell variants from the B-25B through the B-25J. Unfortunately, no 1/32nd scale injection-molded kits of the B-25 have been released.

1/144th SCALE KIT

Only one 1/144th scale plastic model kit of the B-25 has ever been released, although it has been issued under the Crown, Revell, and Academy-Minicraft labels. The most recent release bears the Academy-Minicraft name, but because these two companies are no longer doing business together, it remains to be seen how long this model will be available. Regardless of label, the plastic in all of the issues is the same.

Optional parts are provided so that either a B-25H or a B-25J can be built. The basic shape of the model is fair, but some of the details are incorrect in shape. The gun packs on the forward fuselage are too long, the propeller blades are too wide, and the tail bumper fairing is the wrong shape. There is no representation of the engines inside the nacelles, and the pitot probe is mounted on the wrong wing. A thinner probe should be made from stretched sprue or fine wire, then glued to the correct position on the right wing.

There is no interior for the cockpit or the nose compartment, and as large as these are even in 1/144th scale, at least some basic parts should have been provided. Using some plastic card stock to build interior structures for these areas will significantly improve the appearance of the model. There are also no fixed machine guns for the right side of the nose in the B-25J, and the four machine guns are also missing from the nose piece for the B-25H. In both cases, these machine guns should be added using plastic sprue.

Clear parts are quite thick, and some modelers may want to vacu-form replacements. Surface scribing is

very basic, and small details like the trim tabs on the ailerons are missing.

Overall, this is an average 1/144th scale model, and with a little work, some inaccuracies can be corrected in order to produce a reasonable model of the B-25H or B-25J. In this small scale, it would also be rather simple to "backdate" the model to an earlier B-25B, B-25C, or B-25D.

1/72nd SCALE KITS

Several old releases of B-25 models claim to be in 1/72nd scale. Some are fairly close, while others are not. Kits from Revell, AMT, Frog, Air Lines, Matchbox, Monogram, and Airfix were all inaccurate and lacking in detail. Each of them now has value only to collectors except for the Revell snap-tite kit which is still available and appropriate for beginning modelers.

Clearly, the best place to start in 1/72nd scale is with the B-25s available from Italeri. The B-25B version of this kit has also been released by Testors. Although these are the best models of the Mitchell in 1/72nd scale, each has a number of problems that need to be corrected. The seats in the nose compartment are the wrong shape as is the opening for the crawlway. The seats in the cockpit are also very inaccurate and need to be replaced. There is a bulkhead in the cockpit with a door, but the B-25 did not have a bulkhead in this position. Simply discard this part. Windows in the radio operator's compartment are missing or incorrect depending on the version of the aircraft that is being built, so these too will have to be corrected.

Detailing for the gun turrets is lacking, and the lower turret is very inaccurate. A cover is provided for its opening on versions that did not have this turret. Long exhausts are provided for both nacelles in the kit for the B-25B and B-25C. The B-25B had the long exhaust only on the left nacelle, and the B-25C and B-25D had short exhaust stubs on both engines. The two shrouds for the oil cooler vents on top of the right wing are missing.

The best model of the Mitchell in 1/72nd scale is from Italeri, and it has also been released by Testors. Bob Bartolacci used the kit to build this model of a PBJ-1D in the tri-color paint scheme. (Bartolacci)

The PBJ-1D kit comes with a torpedo installation, but the configuration is incorrect. The model has the torpedo installed with the bomb bay doors open. On the real aircraft, the doors had cutouts that allowed them to remain closed with the torpedo rack installed. Leave the doors closed on the model and cut the rack so that only the exterior part is glued to the closed doors. The PBJ-1D kit also has the radome in place of the lower turret. It should be noted that a few PBJ-1Ds had the tail gun modification that is provided in the kit. For other PBJ-1Cs and PBJ-1Ds, use the basic clear dome instead or install a single machine gun without the gunner's greenhouse. The dual gun packs provided in the PBJ-1D issue are too large, particularly in the vertical dimension.

We strongly recommend using the Italeri/Testors kits for any B-25 model in 1/72nd scale. Because of the inaccuracies present in each of them, we encourage the modeler to carefully study the photographs and drawings in this book so that he can make the necessary corrections and improvements for the specific variant of the Mitchell he is modeling.

1/48th SCALE KITS

Older models of the Mitchell in 1/48th scale include releases by Aurora and Revell. These kits are no longer available, and neither was very accurate or well detailed.

In 1977, Monogram issued a 1/48th scale model of the B-25H, and this was soon followed by two B-25J kits based on the same tooling. One had the standard bombardier's nose, while the other had the solid eight-gun nose. In 1996, after the merger of Revell and Monogram, a ProModeler series kit of a B-25J was released which was based on the original B-25J kit with the glass nose. Additional parts were included for extra machine guns in the nose, a gun gas extractor, and a rearward looking combat camera.

Although these kits have raised panel lines, they are quite accurate and still measure up well by today's standards. Some correcting in the cockpits is required on some issues, but otherwise, these models are excellent.

The B-25H kit had the cut down right seat in the cockpit, but there was no seat in the well next to the cannon for the loader. The co-pilot's yoke and rudder pedals were included, and these should be removed. A large box and foot board should be added in their place as shown on page 57.

When the B-25J kit was issued, the cut down right seat in the cockpit remained, but it should have been replaced with a full seat for the co-pilot. The same problem was found in the release of the B-25J with the solid gun nose. It was not until the ProModeler kit was issued that a correct full seat was provided for the right side in the cockpit. But if these problems in the cockpits are corrected, all issues of these kits are excellent for building B-25H and B-25J variants of the Mitchell.

At press time for this book, Accurate Miniatures was scheduled to begin releasing three kits of earlier Mitchell variants during mid-1999. One is of a B-25B, and markings for all sixteen of the Doolittle raiders are included. A second release can be built as a B-25C or B-25D, while the third kit is of a B-25G. Accurate

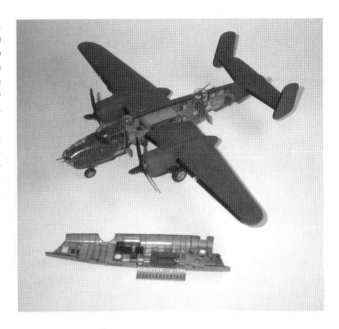

The 1/48th scale kits from Accurate Miniatures are the best B-25 models available. Three releases include a B-25B, a kit that can be built as a B-25C or a B-25D, and a third issue for a B-25G. This B-25B model was built with a portion of the left side of the fuselage cut away to reveal the extensive interior detailing.

Miniatures provided Detail & Scale with a final test shot of one of the kits, and it is clearly the most accurate and detailed model of the Mitchell ever produced. Accurate Miniatures does the most extensive research of any model company as it develops its kits, and this is clearly evident in the final product.

The kits come with plenty of optional parts including the gun positions that were sometimes added at depots or in the field. Standard and strafer noses are provided for the B-25C and B-25D as are external bomb racks and dual gun pods. Bombs of the 100, 250, and 500-pound sizes are included along with depth charges. From nose to tail, internal and external detailing is outstanding throughout.

The one minor problem we found on the test shot was that the wings have the navigation lights on the edge of the tips. The B-25B, C, and D all had two navigation lights on each wing tip with one being on the upper surface and one on the lower. Beginning with B-25G production, the change was made to the single light on the edge of the wing tip as represented in the kit. Some sanding will easily remove the lights for the B-25B, C, or D, and the correct lights can be added from plastic scrap. The model also has the three identification lights under the right wing tip, and these were not added until production of the B-25C and B-25D. They should be filled with modeling putty and sanded out if a B-25B is being modeled.

Otherwise, the Accurate Miniatures B-25s are superb, and they set the standard for detailing and accuracy for the modeling industry.

Jim Roeder contributed to the comments on the 1/72nd and 1/48th scale kits.

IN ACTION SERIES AVAILABLE FROM SQUADRON/SIGNAL PUBLICATIONS

1164 de Havilland D.H.9

1165 B-29 Superfortress

1166 Fokker D. VII

1167 Nieuport Fighters

1168 AH-1 Cobra

1169 La 5/7 Fighters